MJ Gunn
Professor of Mental Health Law
De Montfort University, Leicester

GW00493535

Sex and the law

a brief guide
for staff working
with people
with learning
difficulties

FOURTH EDITION

Published by the Family Planning Association,
2-12 Pentonville Road, London N1 9FP

© M J Gunn, 1996
Previous editions © FPA, 1985, 1987, 1991
Fourth edition May 1996

**British Library Cataloguing in Publication
Data**

A catalogue record for this book is available
from the British Library

ISBN 1 899194 90 8

Designed by Andrew Haig and Associates

Typeset by Intertype

Printed in Great Britain by Acorn Press
Swindon Limited

Contents

Acknowledgements

I would like to express my thanks, in particular, to the co-author of the first edition, Hilary Dixon, who provided considerable assistance in producing a document which was written in understandable English. My thanks also go to Joyce Rosser, not only for co-authoring the second edition but also for being a source of encouragement. As usual the Family Planning Association has been thoroughly supportive in the production of this edition. Finally, but by no means least, I would like to thank my colleagues David Ormerod, Ann Craft and Diane Birch for their expert assistance, support and encouragement.

MJG

Introduction

This publication relates to the law in England and Wales only. The guide, now in its fourth edition, is intended to help staff working with clients with learning difficulties to understand the law regarding sexual behaviour.

There has been a growing awareness of the personal and sexual needs of people with learning difficulties due to the move towards community care and wider acceptance of principles of normalisation. Staff face situations which they have not been trained to deal with, and need help, information and resources to enable them to meet the needs of their clients effectively.

The legal position relating to sexual behaviour is one of the key areas of uncertainty. Staff often do not know what the law is, and when the law has been considered, it leaves many areas of uncertainty. Many social services departments and health authorities have drawn up, or are drawing up, their own policies and guidelines to give staff clearer guidance.

This publication should be treated as an introductory guide. It by no means provides all the answers to the questions that may arise about the law, but it should help to begin to resolve some of the more obvious issues. References have been given which will assist where further clarification is needed. Since the law changes quickly, it is essential that the most up-to-date version of this guide is used. The older it becomes, the more care must be taken in trying to ensure that later developments are taken into account.

Who is the guide for?

The guide is relevant to all professionals working with people with learning difficulties, including:

- social workers

- residential care workers

- hospital and day care staff

- staff from help agencies supporting people with learning difficulties

- sex educators

- health promotion staff.

Notes on using the guide

The guide is separated into sections within chapters for easy reference. It is designed to be read either from cover to cover, or as an introductory reference work. If it is to be used solely as an introductory reference work, it is important to read Chapters 1 and 2 before consulting Chapter 3 which is concerned with specific issues.

The sections into which this guide is divided are referred to as 'section 2.5' or 'section 3.7'. Sections of Acts of Parliament are referred to as 's. 128 of the Mental Health Act 1959' or 's. 27 of the Sexual Offences Act 1956'.

Introductory note on terminology

Terminology in this area is controversial. The term 'people with learning difficulties' is used in this guide when no specific legal meaning is being attributed to the concept. However, the guide is relevant only to those people whose learning difficulty is a product of what can be called a 'mental handicap' or some similar term. This guide is not concerned with people whose learning difficulty has some other cause.

The law only uses the phrase 'learning difficulty' in relation to the provision of special educational facilities to any child whose educational achievement is not as good of that of her/his peers. The phrase, therefore, has no specific legal meaning when the discussion is concerned with adults.

The law's phrases for the people who are the concern of this guide are phrases such as 'mental handicap', 'severe mental handicap', 'mental impairment', 'severe mental impairment', and 'defective', which are all defined at section 2.5 and are used as legally appropriate.

Introductory notes on the law

2.1 **Sources of law**

There is no written constitution in the United Kingdom unlike most other countries of the world. The United Kingdom has a common law system which depends on a combination of statute and case law.

Statute law is derived from Acts of Parliament. Statutes are complex, sometimes ambiguous and often open to various possible interpretations. Case law is established by judgments in individual cases heard in the High Court, the Court of Appeal and the House of Lords – only these courts make decisions which establish precedents binding on lower courts, although decisions of other courts may be influential in certain circumstances. It is rare now for any matter to be based purely on case law. Most judgments are based upon a consideration of the relevant statute and case law. There is considerable statute law, as well as case law, affecting sexual matters (see further Smith & Bailey (1996)).

Law is classified into two broad groups: civil and criminal. It is the latter, in the main, which concerns people's sexual behaviour, making certain activity an offence punishable by the criminal courts. The civil law may, however, have a role to play. In particular, there is a relatively complex argument to support the view that there is an obligation to provide personal and social relationships education, including sex education, for people with learning difficulties if they cannot obtain it otherwise, see, further, Carson (1987) and Gunn (1988). This guide concentrates on the criminal law.

2.2 The process of law

It may be useful to know that an activity of questionable legality may never be tested in the courts, and even if it is, the prosecution case may not be proved or the defendant may be discharged.

The flow diagram indicates the stages that a case must go through if a prosecution is to succeed. At any stage proceedings can end. If relations between clients, parents and staff are good, it is unlikely that a situation would be brought to the attention of the police, unless it were exploitative and/or abusive of one or both of the parties involved.

If it is brought to the attention of the police, they will investigate and decide whether they have sufficient evidence to suggest that there may be a case to answer. They may also decide that, even if there is a case to answer, there is no purpose to be served by pursuing the matter. If the police do believe that the matter should be pursued, the case-file is passed to the Crown Prosecution Service (CPS) which must decide whether or not there is to be a prosecution and thus court action. This decision must be taken in accordance with the Code for Crown Prosecutors.

The Code sets two tests in the decision to prosecute:

i)   'the evidential test'

ii) 'the public interest test'

'Crown Prosecutors must be satisfied that there is enough evidence to provide a "realistic prospect of conviction" against each defendant on each charge ... A realistic prospect of conviction is an objective test. It means that a jury or bench of magistrates, properly directed in accordance with the law, is more likely than not to convict the defendant of the charge alleged.'

(Code for Crown Prosecutors, paras 5.1 and 5.2)

Therefore, the CPS must first assess whether the evidence would be inadmissible or otherwise excluded. Thus, there might be a decision not to prosecute where the complainant would not be competent to give evidence (see section 4.7).

The process of law

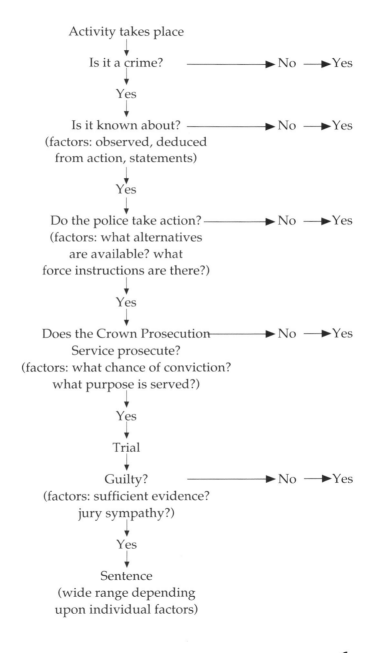

Activity takes place

Is it a crime? ⟶ No ⟶ Yes

Yes

Is it known about? ⟶ No ⟶ Yes
(factors: observed, deduced
from action, statements)

Yes

Do the police take action? ⟶ No ⟶ Yes
(factors: what alternatives
are available? what
force instructions are there?)

Yes

Does the Crown Prosecution ⟶ No ⟶ Yes
Service prosecute?
(factors: what chance of conviction?
what purpose is served?)

Yes

Trial

Guilty? ⟶ No ⟶ Yes
(factors: sufficient evidence?
jury sympathy?)

Yes

Sentence
(wide range depending
upon individual factors)

Secondly, the CPS must determine whether the evidence would be reliable. Generally, it follows that the CPS must also assess the likelihood of the evidence producing a conviction. If there is no supporting evidence other than the evidence of the person with learning difficulties, this is a factor which may weigh against a prosecution, even though there have been major changes to the law on corroboration (see section 4.7). If the person with learning difficulties is unlikely to 'come up to proof', ie is not likely to be sufficiently convincing when giving evidence, this is also a factor weighing against prosecution (see section 4.7).

The 'public interest test' makes clear that not all suspected criminals must 'automatically be the subject of prosecution' (Code for Crown Prosecutors, para 6.1). It is to be considered where the first test has been satisfied and demands a careful balancing of the various relevant factors (Code for Crown Prosecutors, paras 6.2 & 6.3). Some public interest factors are considered in later sections, but it is perhaps reasonable to suggest that, since the purpose of the law is to prevent exploitation or abuse (see *R v Hall* (1987)), it is unlikely that the CPS will bring charges if there is no evidence of such exploitation or abuse.

If the case comes to court, the burden of proof lies with the prosecution, who must prove their case beyond reasonable doubt on the basis of admissible evidence (except for defences under the sexual offences legislation where the burden of proof usually lies with the defence, who must prove the defence on a balance of probabilities on admissible evidence). If there is not sufficient evidence to suggest that the defendant has a case to answer, the case will be dismissed. Even if the case continues, it is possible that the defendant might be found not guilty.

2.3 The law and learning difficulties

There are two ways in which a person with learning difficulties may be affected by the laws on sexual behaviour:

i) Laws which make specific reference to certain categories of people with learning difficulties. These are indicated in

Chapter 3, *The law and specific issues,* and should be read together with the legal definitions (see section 2.5).

ii) Laws which make no specific reference to people with learning difficulties. In these cases all people with learning difficulties will be treated in law the same as the rest of the population.

People with learning difficulties who are competent have the right to make their own decisions in just the same way as anyone else. Thus, it is clear that a person may make their own medical treatment decisions from the age of 16, and even under that age in certain circumstances (see section 3.12). Once a person is 18, they are an adult, and all decisions on any matter can only be taken by them. Thus from at least the age of 18, parents, doctors and other professional people have no legal right to make decisions on their behalf, unless granted specific power to do so (see section 3.14).

In the area of sex law as it affects people with learning difficulties there is very little case law to help with the interpretation of the statutes. The areas of uncertainty are highlighted and suggestions of ways in which the law might be interpreted are indicated. However, at the least, this still leaves staff, at the least, with ethical and moral decisions to make.

In general people with learning difficulties are treated the same as other people in law. This is so, for example, in the context of marriage. Thus a person with learning difficulties may marry with parental consent at the age of 16 and without parental consent at 18, provided only that they have the capacity to marry. It is possible, though, for one party to have the marriage annulled on the ground that the partner suffers from a mental disorder which makes them unfit for marriage. This is unlikely to be successful where the complaining party knew of the mental disorder at the time of the marriage (see section 3.7).

The law on medical consent distinguishes between those people who come within the provisions of the Mental Health Act 1983 (ie people who suffer from 'mental impairment' or 'severe mental impairment' and are compulsorily detained) and others. For those people who are detained under the Mental Health Act 1983, the

question of when the individual must consent to treatment so that
the treatment may be given is answered by reference to ss. 56-64 of
the Act (see the Mental Health Act Code of Practice (1993), Gostin
(1984), Gostin (1986), Hoggett (1990), Jones (1994)). Treatment
which is not *for* the mental disorder from which the detained
patient is suffering cannot be provided under the Mental Health
Act 1983 and so the consent of the patient is necessary if they are an
adult unless they are incompetent to give consent (see sections 3.13
and 3.14). Treatment which is for the mental disorder from which
the detained patient suffers has been widely interpreted in *B v
Croydon H.A.* (1994) (see section 3.14). As regards the treatment
position of people under 18, see sections 3.12-3.13.

2.4 Relevant Acts of Parliament

There are eleven Acts which are directly relevant to the sexual
behaviour of people with learning difficulties. These are:

i) Sexual Offences Act 1956

This deals, amongst other things, with the age of consent for
heterosexual relationships; sexual intercourse with a
'defective'; and indecent assaults committed on either men or
women.

ii) Mental Health Act 1959

Most of this Act has been superseded by the Mental Health Act
1983. However, s.128 dealing with sexual relationships
between staff and 'patients' remains.

iii) Sexual Offences Act 1967

This Act deals with male homosexuality, and includes specific
reference to men who have 'severe mental handicap'.

iv) Mental Health (Amendment) Act 1982

This Act updated parts of the Sexual Offences Acts 1956 and
1967 and the Mental Health Act 1959. Most of it has now been
superseded by the Mental Health Act 1983. The amended
definition of 'defective' and 'severe mental handicap' in the
sexual offences legislation originates from this Act.

v) Mental Health Act 1983

This Act draws together the relevant and extant provisions of both the Mental Health Act 1959 and the Mental Health (Amendment) Act 1982 and supersedes most of those two Acts. Only a small number of people with learning difficulties are covered by the Act. For the majority the same laws apply as for the rest of the population, unless other specific provisions are made (see sections 3.4, 3.5, 3.6, 3.9, 3.10, 3.11, 3.14).

People with learning difficulties can only be covered by the potentially long-term provisions of the Act (in particular relating to admission to hospital for treatment and reception into guardianship, see section 4.8) if they come within the meaning of either 'mental impairment' or 'severe mental impairment'. The short-term provisions (in particular relating to admission to hospital for assessment) apply if the person comes within the wider, generic term: 'mental disorder'. (For more detail on mental health law, see Gostin (1983), Gostin (1986), Hoggett (1990), Jones (1994)).

vi) Sexual Offences Act 1985
This Act made changes in the sentences for certain offences. In particular it made the maximum punishment for indecent assault the same whether it is committed on a man or on a woman.

vii) Education (No. 2) Act 1986
This Act contains a provision, in s. 46, about sex education in county, voluntary and special schools maintained by the local education authority. In such schools, it is the responsibility of the authority, the governing body and the headteacher to 'take such steps as are reasonably practicable to secure that where sex education is given to… pupils … it is given in such a manner as to encourage those pupils to have due regard to moral considerations and the value of family life'. This does not apply directly to adult training centres, etc, but it would appear to be sensible for such places to bear the provision in mind. (This Act also gives governing bodies the right to decide whether or not sex education is included in the curriculum.)

viii) Local Government Act 1986
The Local Government Act 1988, s. 28, introduced a new provision into an existing statute. It created s. 2A of the Local

Government Act 1986. However, since most people know of this provision as 'Section. 28' it will be referred to in the text as 's. 28 of the Local Government Act 1988', although this is not technically accurate.

This provision means that local authorities must not expend finance so as intentionally 'to promote homosexuality or publish material with the intention of promoting homosexuality'. Further, they must not 'promote the teaching in a maintained school of the acceptability of homosexuality as a pretended family relationship'. No restrictions are imposed where the expenditure is for 'the purpose of treating or preventing the spread of disease'.

ix) Sexual Offences Act 1993
This Act abolished the presumption (which was irrebuttable) that a boy under the age of 14 could not have sexual intercourse.

x) Education Act 1993
This Act introduced a number of important changes in relation to sex education in schools which are considered in section 3.11.

xi) Criminal Justice and Public Order Act 1994
This Act made some significant changes in the law relating to:

– rape by making clear that there is no marital exemption so a husband can be found guilty of rape where he has non-consensual sexual intercourse with his wife, applying the offence of rape to men as well as women and applying the offence of rape to anal as well as vaginal intercourse (see sections 3.2, 3.4 & 3.10)

– buggery (see section 3.10)

– the age of consent for male homosexual activity was lowered to 18 (see section 3.10)

– evidence, in particular as regards the law relating to corroboration (see section 4.7).

2.5 Legal definitions of learning difficulties

A study of these Acts shows the change in terminology used over the years to categorise people who are now described as having learning difficulties and/or mental handicap. It is important to understand the definitions used in each Act and to remember that these terms have a specific legal meaning which may not be the same as the meanings given to them in general or professional conversation. It should be noted here that the same or similar concepts may also appear in other legislation (eg 'severe mental handicap' and 'mental handicap' are also used in the Juries Act 1974 as amended) (see further, section 2.6).

i) 'Defective'

This word is used in the Sexual Offences Act 1956. It is now defined in Schedule 3 to the Mental Health (Amendment) Act 1982 and means:

'a state of arrested or incomplete development of mind which includes severe impairment of intelligence and social functioning'.

The definition is quite similar to that of 'severe subnormality' in the old Mental Health Act 1959, although in some respects significantly different. It is the same as the definition of 'severe mental handicap' in the Sexual Offences Act 1967 and in the Juries Act 1974 (see ii. below). It is also exactly the same as the definition of 'severe mental impairment' in the Mental Health Act 1983 less the requirement of 'abnormally aggressive or seriously irresponsible conduct on the part of the person concerned.' (see iv. below).

ii) 'Severe mental handicap'

This phrase is used in the Sexual Offences Act 1967 and has the same meaning as 'defective'. It does have other statutory usages, such as in the Juries Act 1974.

iii) 'Mental disorder'

This term, in the Mental Health Act 1983, is defined as meaning 'mental illness, arrested or incomplete development of mind, psychopathic disorder and any other disorder or disability of mind'. This covers all forms of mental handicap as understood by care professionals.

A person does not suffer from mental disorder 'by reason only of promiscuity or other immoral conduct, sexual deviancy or dependence on alcohol or drugs.'

iv) 'Mental impairment' / 'severe mental impairment'
These are the terms used in the Mental Health Act 1983. They were introduced to refer to the small minority of people with mental handicap who need to be detained in a mental hospital long term on the basis solely of their mental handicap. Part of the justification for such detention is that the person is also abnormally aggressive or seriously irresponsible (ie unable to be responsible) whereas the great majority of people with learning difficulties are not abnormally aggressive or seriously irresponsible. They therefore do not need to be and are not subject to long-term compulsory Mental Health Act powers.

The distinction between mental impairment and severe mental impairment is one of degree of impairment. The impairment of intelligence and social functioning must be 'significant' for the former and 'severe' for the latter. This distinction is important because there are differences in the grounds upon which a person can be detained or have her/his detention renewed (see Gunn, 1986).

It should be remembered that 'learning difficulties' does also have a legal meaning, although the phrase is not used in that sense in this guide. The Education Act 1993 uses the phrase to describe those children who have significantly greater difficulty in learning than the majority of children of the same age, whatever the cause of that difficulty may be.

2.6 Labelling and classification

Since the label or classification that is used to describe a person may have significant effects upon their freedom of sexual expression and the availability of sex education, considerable care needs to be taken in any labelling or classification process to avoid unfortunate and unnecessary consequences.

In much of what follows it will become clear that the sexual freedoms of those people classified as 'defective' (or 'severely mentally handicapped') are highly restricted. Yet there is no general agreement on how people are defined as 'defective'.

As a rough guide, severe impairment of intelligence is often taken to mean those with an IQ below 50. However, limiting assessment of impairment of intelligence to the results of an IQ test would appear to be assuming an inappropriately limited definition of intelligence.

With any classification it still needs to be considered whether or not the client's social functioning is also severely impaired. Thus, whilst perhaps also taking into account the results of adaptive behaviour tests, a careful assessment of the various forms of social functioning must also be made. Social functioning presumably includes such matters as: ability to care for oneself; personal hygiene; personal and social (perhaps sexual) relationships with others.

If a client's notes or files contain a descriptive phrase like 'severely mentally handicapped', it will be assumed that that client is a 'defective' and arguing against such an assumption may not be easy. Thus care needs to be taken in placing any descriptive phrases on such files or in such notes.

In *R v Hall* (1987), where the victim was a woman with a 'mental age of 9 or 10 and an IQ of 53' who was a defective according to the jury, the Court of Appeal decided that the words defining 'defective' were 'words of the ordinary English language'. Whether someone is a defective is to be measured by 'the standards of normal persons' and is to be decided by the jury. Expert evidence could be heard to establish intelligence, but probably not to establish whether someone was a 'defective'. Indeed, it is not necessary to have any expert evidence (*R v Robbins* (1988)). Here the Court of Appeal decided that the direction of the judge permitting the jury to decide whether the complainant had a severe mental handicap without expert evidence was unobjectionable. The jury had found that the complainant who 'was simple minded with a mental age well below his true years' did not suffer from a severe mental handicap.

These decisions have little effect in day-to-day matters where it is right to depend upon professional assessments. More notice would have to be taken if there were many decisions which indicated that the jury and professional perceptions were markedly different in deciding whether someone was a 'defective'. It is unlikely that there will be such an increase in the number of cases reaching court.

The law and specific issues

3.1 The general law on sexual intercourse: the age of consent

Sixteen year old women and men may enter into sexual relationships with members of the opposite sex. Women may enter lesbian relationships at 16 (see section 3.9). Men may enter into homosexual relationships at 18 (see section 3.10; note that until the change made by the Criminal Justice and Public Order Act 1994, the age limit had been 21). The old rule that a boy was presumed to be incapable of sexual intercourse below the age of 14 was abolished by the Criminal Justice Act 1993, thus a boy younger than that age may now be guilty of any of the offences involving sexual intercourse. Sixteen year olds, female or male, may marry with parental consent and may change their doctor or decide on their own medical treatment without parental knowledge (see section 3.12 on medical treatment). A couple may marry without parental consent at 18.

('Parents' here and elsewhere in this publication includes other people with parental responsibility and the guardians of minors (see Lyon (1993), Chapter 4). Guardians of minors should not be confused with guardians under the Mental Health Act 1983 who perform a different function and are not, therefore, included in the word 'parents'.)

3.2 The general law on sexual intercourse: sexual intercourse and rape

Under the Sexual Offences Act 1956 there are a number of offences which are designed for the protection of all women with or without learning difficulties. These include rape, that, is non-consensual sexual intercourse, as well as a number of offences which are specific to people with learning difficulties.

The Criminal Justice and Public Order Act 1994 amended the definition of rape by:

i) making it clear that a husband can be guilty of the rape of his wife where she does not consent to sexual intercourse

ii) extending the law of rape to cover anal intercourse with a woman

iii) extending the law of rape to cover anal intercourse with a man.

Both the latter two were only the offence of buggery under the unamended Sexual Offences Act 1956. The offence of rape is now defined in the amended section 1 of the Sexual Offences Act 1956 as follows:

'(**1**) *It is an offence for a man to rape a woman or another man.*

(**2**) *A man commits rape if:*

(**a**) *he has sexual intercourse with a person (whether vaginal or anal) who at the time of the intercourse does not consent to it; and*

(**b**) *at the time he knows that the person does not consent to the intercourse or is reckless as to whether that person consents to it.'*

The law defines sexual intercourse as demanding penetration by a man's penis (Sexual Offences Act 1956, s.44). It does not include other forms of vaginal or anal penetration. Penile penetration need not include ejaculation.

At one time there was a rule that a husband could not be guilty of rape even though he had had non-consensual sexual intercourse with his wife. However, this was abolished by the House of Lords in *R v R* (1991). This decision was confirmed by Parliament, since the new definition of rape in the amended Sexual Offences Act 1956, section 1 (reproduced above) makes no mention of the word 'unlawful'. Where the word 'unlawful' is used in the sexual offences legislation, it means 'outside marriage'. Thus, a man may be criminally liable for raping his wife.

A man has never had an exemption or immunity from liability for committing other offences against his wife. So it has always been possible for a husband to be guilty of committing an indecent assault on his wife (see *R v Kowalski* (1987)). This is still the law.

For rape, the sexual intercourse must be non-consensual. That is, rape is committed where the woman (or a man) does not consent. Force, fear or fraud does not need to be exercised on the woman (or a man); a simple lack of consent is sufficient to mean that a man having sexual intercourse with a woman (or a man) is committing the offence of rape (see Temkin (1987), pp60-71). Consent, according to the Court of Appeal in *R v Olugboja* (1981), is to be given its ordinary meaning, emphasising that it is not the same as mere submission. Thus what is required is a decision on the part of the woman (or man) that she (or he) wishes to have sex. In order to consent she (or he) must understand the 'nature of the act'. Exactly how much knowledge and appreciation of what sexual intercourse involves is a matter of debate. It may simply require knowledge that sex involves penetration by the male sexual organ or that the act is of a sexual nature. On the other hand, it may require awareness on the part of the woman (or man) of the significance of sexual intercourse and its implications for her (or him). The advantage of the former requirement is that it means that many more women (and men) can consent; the advantage of the latter is that it is more likely to protect some women (and men) from exploitation and abuse. It would seem that, at least with regard to young girls, the latter approach is generally adopted by the courts (*R v Harling* (1938), *R v Howard* (1965); see generally Temkin (1987), pp71-73).

If a person is deceived into consenting to sexual intercourse, that is the consent is obtained by fraud, the consent may be still valid so preventing a conviction for rape. Fraud, in two cases, makes the consent invalid and so the appropriate offence is that of rape:

i)   The person is deceived as to the 'nature and quality of the act'. She (or he) believes that what is happening is not sexual intercourse (eg where the person is led to believe that the man is to perform a surgical operation (*R v Flattery* (1877)). Deceit as to some other factor, however important it might appear, does not vitiate consent (eg a prostitute's consent was still valid even though the man led her to believe that she would be paid, he never intended to pay her and did not pay her, so there could be no conviction for rape (*R v Linekar* (1995))).

ii) The person is led to believe, wrongly, that the man is her husband or her or his partner (*R v Elbekkay* (1995)). It may be that this case means that fraud as to identification will always vitiate the apparent consent, or the woman may have to be deceived as to his identity, believing that he is her (long standing) sexual partner.

It is an offence, contrary to s.3 of the Sexual Offences Act 1956, to 'procure a woman, by false pretences or false representations, to have sexual intercourse in any part of the world.' Thus an offence will have been committed where consent is obtained by fraud. This offence applies in relation to women only.

Rape is not an absolute offence (see section 3.3), but is an offence which requires that the man knew that the woman (or man) did not consent or was reckless whether she consented (Sexual Offences Act 1956, s. 1 (as amended), and see Temkin (1987), pp76-91). The learning difficulties of the male defendant may be relevant in assessing this issue and expert evidence can be heard to assess the IQ of a man with learning difficulties or mental handicap (*R v Masih* (1986)).

It is also an offence, contrary to s.2 of the Sexual Offences Act 1956 for 'a person to procure a woman, by threats or intimidation, to have sexual intercourse in any part of the world'.

It is an offence, contrary to section 4 of the Sexual Offences Act 1956, for 'a person to apply or administer to, or cause to be taken by, a woman any drug, matter or thing with intent to stupefy or overpower her so as thereby to enable any man to have unlawful sexual intercourse with her.'

In either of these instances the activity may mean that she is not consenting, but, even if she is consenting, the offences are committed provided sexual intercourse is secured by threats, intimidation or drugs (see Smith & Hogan (1992), pp460-462).

3.3 The general law on sexual intercourse: under-age sex

Under the Sexual Offences Act 1956 there are two offences concerning a male who has sexual intercourse with a girl. The first is when the girl is under 13 and the second is when the girl is under 16. These offences are committed even if the girl consents to sexual intercourse (*R v Harling* (1938)). It is an absolute offence, under the Sexual Offences Act 1956, s.5, for a man to have sexual intercourse with a girl under the age of 13. An absolute offence is one for which no defence of mistaking the age of the girl is allowed.

The second offence, under the Sexual Offences Act 1956, s.6, is concerned with any girl under the age of 16, but is most likely to apply to girls who are more than 13 years of age. Under this offence, the male may be able to claim in his defence (having to prove it on a balance of probabilities), and thus be adjudged not guilty:

i) that he believed himself to be validly married to the girl and had reasonable cause for that belief. (This situation could arise where a marriage had been contracted in a country with a lower age of marriage);

ii) that he believed the girl to be 16 or over and had reasonable cause for that belief. This applies only if he is under 24 and has not previously been charged with a like offence.

The male may be of any age. There used to be an irrebuttable presumption that a boy under the age of 14 could not have sexual intercourse, but this was abolished by the Criminal Justice Act 1993.

Where both the male and the female are young, the male still commits the offence, even where he is younger than she. In practice prosecutions are rare if there is no evidence of exploitation. The old version of the Code for Crown Prosecutors provided that

'Whenever two or more persons have participated in the offence in circumstances rendering both or all liable to prosecution the Crown Prosecutor should take into account each person's age, the relative ages of the participants and whether or not there was any element of seduction or corruption when deciding whether, and if so in respect of whom, proceedings should be instituted.'

The current Code for Crown Prosecutors no longer deals specifically with this issue. In addition to the general factors relating to the discretion to prosecute (see the Code and section 2.2), the current Code states that the following factors should be considered in determining whether a prosecution would be in the public interest:

'The relationship between the victim and the public interest

6.7 The Crown Prosecution Service acts in the public interest, not just in the interests of any one individual. But Crown Prosecutors must always think very carefully about the interests of the victim, which are an important factor, when deciding where the public interest lies.

Youth offenders
6.8 Crown prosecutors must consider the interests of a youth when deciding whether it is in the public interest to prosecute. The stigma of a conviction can cause very serious harm to the prospects of a youth offender or a young adult. Young offenders can sometimes be dealt with without going to court. But Crown prosecutors should not avoid prosecuting simply because of the defendant's age. The seriousness of the offence or the offender's past behaviour may make prosecution necessary.'

The Sexual Offences Act 1956 does not refer to a woman having sexual intercourse with a boy under 16. However, she could be charged with indecent assault (see section 3.9).

The Sexual Offences Act 1956 gives the same protection to a girl under 16 who has learning difficulties as it does to any other girl.

3.4 The specific law relating to people with learning difficulties: sexual intercourse and rape

The general law on sexual intercourse applies to people with learning difficulties, so it recognises that a woman with learning difficulties can, not only in fact, but also in law be raped. If a woman with learning difficulties can consent to sexual intercourse (which, since the amendments of the Criminal Justice and Public Order Act 1994, may be vaginal or anal sex; see section 3.2), a man having sex with her without her consent is committing rape, provided he either knew she was not consenting or was reckless as to whether she was consenting. If the woman with learning difficulties cannot actually consent, a man having sex with her is committing the offence of rape because the woman can provide no consent.

As considered further at section 3.2, what matters is the meaning of consent. If a low standard is adopted, requiring simply an understanding of penile penetration and that it is a sexual act, then many women with learning difficulties will be able to provide consent. If a higher standard is adopted, requiring an awareness of the significance of sexual intercourse and its implications for her, fewer women with learning difficulties will be able to consent. The advantage of the former approach is that many more women with learning difficulties can enjoy sexual relationships. The advantage of the latter approach is that it protects more women with learning difficulties, including women who do not also fall within the definition of 'defective' (see below), from exploitation and abuse (see Temkin (1987), pp71-72). The same principles apply where the sexual intercourse is anal. As pointed out in section 3.2., a man may now, in law, be the victim of rape, and the implications of this for men with learning difficulties are considered below at section 3.10).

In addition, the law (the Sexual Offences Act 1956) makes specific reference to 'defective' women and sexual intercourse. It also makes specific reference to 'defective' women and men and sexual acts not necessarily amounting to sexual intercourse (see section 3.9). So it is an offence for a man to have unlawful sexual intercourse with a woman who is a defective (s.7); for anyone to procure a woman defective to have unlawful sexual intercourse with any man or men (s.9); or for anyone to take a defective woman away from the care of her parent with the purpose that she shall have unlawful sexual intercourse with a man (s.21).

All these offences require sexual intercourse, which for these offences must be vaginal but is complete upon penetration and therefore does not demand ejaculation or the completion of sex by the man. It will also be seen that all these offences require that sexual intercourse to be 'unlawful'. This word, in these offences, means 'outside the bounds of matrimony' (Smith (1991), Law Commission (1990b), paragraph 2.6). This is still the law, despite the change to the law of rape making clear that a husband can be guilty of rape when he has sexual intercourse with his wife who was not consenting (see section 3.2). Consequently, a man who is married to a woman who is a 'defective' does not commit the offence contrary to s.7 of the Sexual Offences Act 1956 when he has sexual intercourse with her. Of course, if she does not consent, he may have committed the offence of rape (see section 3.2).

The law also deals with men suffering from 'severe mental handicap' and homosexual relationships (Sexual Offences Act 1967) (see section 3.10). All other men aged 18 or over are able to enter into homosexual relationships in private. Homosexual relationships in the armed forces are now only disciplinary offences which may lead to dismissal, but are no longer crimes. There is no law making specific reference to homosexual relationships between women (see section 3.10). A woman may enter a homosexual relationship at 16; before that age she cannot in law give the consent necessary to prevent the act being an indecent assault (see sections 3.9, 3.10).

'Defective' has been redefined by the Mental Health (Amendment) Act 1982 (see section 2.5).

In practice prosecutions for having sexual relationships with someone who is a defective are rare for a number of reasons, including that it may be difficult for the lay person to recognise the degree of impairment of intelligence and social functioning which someone who is a defective has. In all these offences, therefore, there is a 'get out' clause, that is, a person is not guilty of they can show that they did not know and had no reasons to suspect the person to be a defective (see section 3.9).

The purpose of these laws is, or should be, to protect women with learning difficulties from exploitation and abuse. If there is no exploitation it may be acceptable to enable her (or him) to have sexual intercourse. (The same points can be made in relation to women having sex with men in the context of the offence of indecent assault (see section 3.9).)

This point needs to be made tentatively, because it depends upon the discretion being exercised not to prosecute (as to the discretion, see section 2.2). Specific relevant guidance was offered in the old version of the Code for Crown Prosecutors which stated

'Whenever two or more persons have participated in the offence in circumstances rendering both or all liable to prosecution the Crown Prosecutor should take into account each person's age, the relative ages of the participants and whether or not there was any element of seduction or corruption when deciding whether, and if so in respect of whom, proceedings should be instituted.'

Whilst this guidance does not appear in the current Code for Crown Prosecutors, it is likely still to represent suitable guidance on the exercise of the prosecution discretion.

3.5 The specific law relating to people with learning difficulties: sexual intercourse in certain premises

S.27 of the Sexual Offences Act 1956 applies to most staff. It makes it an offence for 'the owner. occupier or anyone who has or acts in the management or control of any premises to induce or knowingly suffer a woman who is a defective to resort to or be on those premises for the purpose of having unlawful sexual intercourse with men or a particular man.'

This is undoubtedly a very wide offence. It might well be a major obstacle in permitting the continuation of a valuable sexual relationship in such premises. However, the alternative to permitting such a relationship is unlikely to be to stop it, but rather to force the couple to find alternative venues at which to have sex. Such venues may not be available or may be highly unsuitable for a variety of reasons.

The sexual intercourse must be 'unlawful'. If the couple are married, the sexual intercourse is not 'unlawful' and so the staff commit no offence under s.27. (as to the meaning of 'unlawful, see section 3.4).

The member of staff must be the owner or occupier or be involved in the management or control of the premises to fall within s. 27. Most members of staff will not be the owners of the premises. However, most members of staff will either have the ability to exclude people from the premises in view of their control over them, or share, or assist in the running of the premises, undertaking duties which are not purely menial or routine. Consequently, they will either be occupiers or be involved in the management or control of the premises (see Fortson (1988), pp142-147, for a discussion of similar concepts in an offence concerned with drugs offences in premises).

The requirement that the member of staff must 'knowingly' allow a defective woman to be on the premises for the purpose of unlawful sexual intercourse is likely to be easily satisfied in most cases, except where there is a casual relationship. Knowledge is satisfied by the staff either being fully aware of such relationships taking place through actual knowledge or shutting their eyes to the obvious. It is possible that the courts might interpret the phrase 'knowingly suffer' to mean cause or encourage (*R v Chainey* (1914)). Since most situations are ones where staff know what is happening, but do not actively encourage it, this possible interpretation could be quite important. However, other courts have taken the view that, in other offences, 'suffer' simply means failing to act and 'permit' means doing something to allow the activity to happen (Fortson (1988)).

However, although this offence does appear to be of considerable significance as a possible obstacle in permitting normal sexual relationships in a variety of types of accommodation, there are three points to consider:

i) a case would first have to be reported before any action could commence

ii) there would be no automatic prosecution, because it is anticipated that the prosecution discretion would be exercised in favour of no action where the relationship is a valuable one for the couple and which cannot be described as either exploitative or abusive of either party

iii) this offence is, it would seem, more concerned with prostitution or, at least, promiscuity than with relationships. It would have to be proved that a defective was on the premises 'for the purpose of' sexual intercourse. So it might be argued that if the woman was in the place which was her home, she was not there 'for the purpose of' sexual intercourse, but to lie there. This argument would be countered by the proposition that people may have more than one purpose in what they do.

3.6 The specific law relating to people with learning difficulties: sexual relationships with staff

Under s.128 of the Mental Health Act 1959 it is an offence for a male member of staff or manager of a hospital or mental nursing home to have unlawful sexual intercourse with a woman 'who is for the time receiving treatment for mental disorder' or is an out-patient at the hospital or home. It is also an offence for 'a man to have unlawful sexual intercourse with a woman who is a mentally disordered patient and who is subject to guardianship or is otherwise in his custody and care' under the Mental Health Act 1983, or in National Health Service premises, or in 'Part III' accommodation (National Assistance Act 1948. The Sexual Offences Act 1967 also makes it an offence for a male member of staff to commit acts of gross indecency on male patients.

The phrase 'mental disorder' (see section 2.5) means that all clients with learning difficulties, however severe, are protected by the above offences, provided the clients fall within the other elements of the offences are satisfied.

The DHSS Memorandum on the Mental Health Act 1983 (1987) requires that 'where there is reason to believe that an offence has been committed the Chief Constable should be informed as soon as possible.' The Memorandum indicates that it is then for the police in consultation with the patient's doctor to decide what is the best course of action. The Crown Prosecution Service is not mentioned only because it was not in operation at the time this part of the Memorandum was written. The CPS will be involved in the decision whether to prosecute.

By law, there can be no prosecution for these offences without the consent of the Director of Public Prosecutions (DPP). This consent does not have to be given by the DPP in person but is delegated.

There is no equivalent law concerning female members of staff or managers. Female staff could be charged with an indecent assault (see section 3.9). Sexual relationships between female staff and patients could be construed as ill-treatment which is a separate criminal offence under s.127 of the Mental Health Act 1983 (see section 4.6 and *Encyclopaedia of social services law & practice*; Gunn (1989)).

3.7   Marriage and divorce

A person with learning difficulties who is aged 18 or over may marry, without parental consent, just like any other person over 18. The officiant (registrar or appropriate minister) must be satisfied that they understand the nature of the proposed undertaking. The courts regard the 'contract' of marriage as a relatively simple form of agreement or commitment. Thus it is relatively easy for the officiant to be satisfied that a person has sufficient understanding.

There is no law specifically restricting the right of people with learning difficulties to marry. There is no rule of law which states that a person with learning difficulties cannot marry, nor is there a rule of law which states that a person who is a 'defective' within the meaning of the Sexual Offences Act 1956 cannot marry. The Marriage Act 1983 merely allows for the possibility that a person who is a detained patient may be allowed to marry in hospital.

If the officiant has any doubt about the capacity of a person with learning difficulties to marry, they may ask a professional person to provide a statement indicating whether that professional is of the view that the person with learning difficulties has the requisite consent. It is also possible that someone could 'enter a caveat with the Superintendent Registrar against the issue of a certificate or licence for the marriage of a named person' (Marriage Act 1949, s.29 as modified by the Marriage (Registrar General's Licences Act 1970, s.5). This would mean that the Registrar would have to examine the matter before marrying the couple. A doctor or anyone else could instigate this procedure. No caveat should be entered unless there are good grounds for doing so, because if the caveat was found to be frivolous, the person entering it could be liable for the costs of the Registrar and damages to the couple. Where the couple are to marry in church, the objection would be to the banns.

A person between the ages of 16 and 18 with learning difficulties would have to ask and obtain the permission of her/his parent, in the same way as a non-handicapped teenager.

The law does recognise that mental disorder may make a person unfit for marriage. If that can be established by one of the partners, they can have the marriage annulled. This would be an extremely difficult procedure to pursue, especially where that partner knew of the disorder at the time of the marriage (Cretney & Masson (1990)).

Thus a person with learning difficulties who is aged 18 or more can, in law, make their own decision to marry without parental consent or professional permission. In practice, they may need considerable help. One problem which can arise when a couple (both with learning difficulties and supported by different local authorities) wish to marry is which local authority will support and house them. This may be a practical factor in delaying marriage.

The law relating to divorce treats people with learning difficulties the same as anyone else.

3.8 Indecent exposure

There are three categories of indecent exposure:

i)   **Common law:** according to the leading criminal law textbook 'it is a common law [offence] to commit an act outraging public decency in public and in such a way that more than one person sees, or is at least able to see, the act.' (Smith and Hogan (1992), p 474).

This is a very wide offence, because:

–   'in public', in this offence, means where the public go, whether or not they are supposed to

–   two people do not actually have to see the act

–   nobody has to be disgusted or annoyed

–   no sexual motive is necessary

–   no desire to insult or annoy needs to be established

–   it can be committed by either male or female.

It may be, however, that no offence is committed where the people seeing the exposure either consent (eg in nudist camps) or where the person exposing herself or himself believes that they would consent.

ii)   **Vagrancy Act 1824:** this states, at s.4, that 'every person wilfully, openly, lewdly and obscenely exposing his person to insult any female ... shall be deemed a rogue and a vagabond.' In this context, 'person' means 'penis'.

iii)   **Local Acts and byelaws:** there are a wide variety of these which would need to be checked for each area, through the local town hall.

The charge of indecent exposure may well be used against people with learning difficulties, unless education programmes providing information about appropriate behaviour are available, which enable people to know what is socially acceptable and what is not.

3.9 Indecent assault

Indecent assault under the Sexual Offences Act 1956 can be committed on either a woman (s.14) or a man (s.15). The offence is the same in both sections. The offence can be committed by either a man or a woman. Whether the assault is committed on a man or a woman, the maximum sentence has been the same since the Sexual Offences Act 1985. The maximum sentence is 10 years' imprisonment.

There are three requirements for the offence of indecent assault:

i)   an assault: this means that the victim must have something done to them by a man or a woman (ie some form of contact), or that they apprehend that something will be done in the very near future. Technically, an assault covers both an assault and a battery. Battery requires that there be actual unlawful personal violence and an assault requires that the victim apprehend immediate unlawful personal violence. In this context 'violence' merely means contact or touching. 'Apprehend' does not require that the victim be scared or frightened.

Ordinarily an assault will involve something actually done (technically, a battery will be committed). It can vary from relatively minor assaults (eg touching a woman's breasts without her consent) to very serious ones (eg forcible vaginal penetration with a bottle). But it is important to be aware that making the other person apprehend or anticipate the contact in the immediate or near future is sufficient for an assault, so placing a hand near a woman's vagina may well amount to an assault.

ii)   the assault must be indecent: the requirement of indecency has been described by the House of Lords (*R v Court* (1988)) as follows:

'... conduct that right-thinking people will consider an affront to the sexual modesty of a woman.'

'... [would] right-minded persons ... consider the conduct indecent or not.'

'... [was] what occurred ... so offensive to contemporary standards of modesty and privacy as to be indecent.'

The House of Lords felt that some acts are inherently indecent, such as removing a woman's clothing against her will, whereas some acts are only capable of being indecent, such as spanking a 13 year old girl on the bottom when fully dressed (as happened in *R v Court*). When the act is only capable of being indecent, the explanation that the defendant gives of their acts will help to determine whether or not the act was indecent.

Something like a vaginal examination for genuine medical purposes might well appear, at first sight, to be an act which is inherently indecent. However, this can only be determined if it is the case that 'right-minded' people would regard it as indecent, and it ought not to be resolved by an unconsidered first impression. It is, therefore, quite likely to be the case that such an examination, applying the proper test, would not be regarded as indecent. Likewise, where a person is taught to manage her own menstruation by a hands-on method, it is submitted that the activity involved would not be regarded as indecent. Similarly also, it may be the case that teaching masturbation by direct method may not be regarded as indecent, although this obviously cannot be confidently asserted. In many instances, of course, the defence of consent is also available, so that if the act is regarded as indecent, it is still not an offence. However, where the person upon whom the act is being performed is a person who is a 'defective' within the meaning of the Sexual Offences Act 1956, they are not, in law, be allowed to give consent (see below). Thus, the question of whether the act is indecent may be crucially important.

iii) an intention indecently to assault: if a person's intention is not indecently to assault, they cannot be guilty. It may be the case that this will permit a person to argue that, since they were providing an essential ability (managing menstruation, learning masturbation) in a professionally appropriate fashion, no such intention was present. Indeed Lord Ackner in *R v Court* states '... any evidence which tends to explain the reasons for the defendant's conduct ... would be relevant to establish whether or not he intended to commit, not only an assault, but an indecent one.'

It is submitted that a member of staff may rely upon both the meaning of indecency and the requirement that the act must be done with an indecent intention to argue that certain activities (primarily teaching someone to manage with menstruation and other matters of personal hygiene, and teaching masturbation) are not indecent assaults.

Non-consensual assault
Ordinarily consent will mean that no offence has been committed. By statute, however, girls and boys under the age of 16 cannot in law consent, whatever their actual level of understanding of the issues may be.

A 'defective' man or woman cannot in law give consent (see sections 2.5, 3.4, 3.10). If the actor (the person committing the act) did not know and had no reason to suspect that the other person was a 'defective', they cannot be guilty of an indecent assault because of that incapacity to consent. In *R v Blair* (1995) the Court of Appeal indicated that there was evidence on which a jury, properly directed, could arrive at the conclusion that a person knew or had reason to suspect that a young woman was a 'defective'. The two had shared a short car journey with some conversation taking place; he had spent time at his flat showing her around and getting her a drink; and they had sat on a bed where he inserted his fingers in her vagina causing her hymen to be ruptured. They were together for some 20-25 minutes before the alleged assault and there was evidence from the victim's mother and GP and from the college the victim attended about her 'manifest problems in understanding and communication'. The Court of Appeal therefore refused leave for Blair to appeal against his conviction for indecent assault. His sentence, however, was reduced from four years to 21 months' imprisonment, in part because the sentence for an indecent assault on a person who is a defective, it was decided, should take into account that, whilst the maximum for that offence is 10 years' imprisonment, the maximum sentence for having unlawful sexual intercourse with a defective is 2 years' imprisonment.

In some additional circumstances, regardless of the victim's capacity, the courts have held that a person cannot consent to certain actions however willing they may be (eg a 17 year old girl being whipped for sexual gratification, *R v Donovan* (1934)). The House of Lords has confirmed in *R v Brown* (1994) that the correct approach is, first, to determine whether actual bodily harm was caused or intended, and, secondly, if it was, then to assess whether there is any public interest in the activity to permit it despite the actual bodily harm. Thus, the whipping in *R v Donovan* would involve the causing of actual bodily harm and there was no public interest in allowing such activity for sexual gratification with a relatively young woman. In *R v Brown* the homosexual, sado-masochistic acts would involve the causing of actual bodily harm and, again, the court took the view that there was no public interest in allowing this sort of activity. This issue seems not to affect the general proposition that there are circumstances in which teaching about menstruation and/or masturbation to a person with learning difficulties who cannot learn for themselves is lawful, since there should be no actual bodily harm either caused or intended and also that there is a very clear public interest in favour of providing such teaching.

It should be remembered that there is no 'marital exemption or immunity' for a husband which would enable him to avoid conviction if he had indecently assaulted his wife without her consent (see section 3.4).

It is not an offence for a woman to have sex with a man (even without his consent or where he is a 'defective'). However, it is likely that she will indecently touch him in the course of having sex. Therefore, she is likely to commit an indecent assault on him. This is no offence where he consents, but he cannot consent, in law, if he is under 16 or is a 'defective'.

Clearly this offence is of concern to people with learning

difficulties and to staff working with them. However, indecent assault is only likely to be relevant in circumstances where not only the words of the offence are satisfied, but also the prosecuting authorities are satisfied that it is appropriate to take action (see section 2.2).

Consequently, it is most likely that legal action with regard to indecent assault will be taken in the following types of cases, and especially where the victim not only has learning difficulties, but also satisfies the definition of 'defective' (see section 2.5):

i)   where two women are involved in a sexual relationship, and there is some evidence of exploitation of one by the other

ii)   where a member of staff is inappropriately helping (eg doing it outside the context of a personal and social relationships programme or for the prurient interests of the member of staff) a person with learning difficulties to masturbate

iii) where a member of staff is for prurient reasons helping a person with learning difficulties learn about personal hygiene

iv)   where a female member of staff is having a sexual relationship with a man with learning difficulties.

It is, of course, possible that legal action could at least be instituted where members of staff are acting appropriately, but it is suggested that the arguments propounded in this section should enable a conviction to be avoided.

3.10   Homosexuality

The only offence which can be concerned with lesbianism is that of indecent assault (see section 3.9). Consequently, acts of lesbianism, which involve an indecent assault, are legal provided both women consent and neither are under the age of 16. A 'defective' woman cannot in law, however, provide consent (see section 3.9 for further discussion of this issue).

When the concern is with male homosexuality, there are a number of offences which may be relevant, including the following which are the main offences:

i) Indecent assault may have been committed (see section 3.9).

ii) The Sexual Offences Act 1956, s.13, makes all acts of gross indecency illegal. According to Honore (1978), 'the phrase "gross indecency" suggests a contrast with ordinary decency. Perhaps it would be an act of ordinary but not gross indecency for a man to kiss another man with sexual intentions or in a way that had sexual overtones.' The act of gross indecency may be committed in public or private. Consent is not a defence to this offence, except for in the circumstances considered below.

iii) The Sexual Offences Act 1956, s. 12, makes buggery an offence. Buggery may be committed by any person with another person (either a man or a woman) or with an animal. Consent is not a defence to this offence, except in the circumstances considered below.

iv) Since the amendments introduced by the Criminal Justice and Public Order Act 1994, a man may now be the victim of a rape, which is committed where a man has anal intercourse with another man without the latter's consent (see further, section 3.2 for a full discussion of the elements of the offence).

However, the Sexual Offences Act 1967 legalises male homosexual acts in certain circumstances. The phrase 'homosexual acts' applies to the offences of gross indecency and buggery. Such acts are lawful provided both men consent and the act takes place in private. In addition, both men must be at least 18 years of age. The age of consent was lowered from 21 by the Criminal Justice and Public Order Act 1994, s.145. An indecent assault is lawful if the person consents to it (see section 3.9) and no rape is committed where the man consents to the anal intercourse. For these two offences, consent is usually a defence, whereas for the two 'homosexual acts' offences, consent is not usually a defence, but, as indicated, is a defence in the circumstances specified within the Sexual Offences Act 1967.

The 1967 Act makes clear that certain circumstances mean that an act does not take place in private. If there are more than two people present, the act does not take place in private, even if it takes place in the bedroom of a private house of one of the participants. Further, the act does not take place in private if it happens in a public lavatory. The 1967 Act itself gives no further guidance as to when an act takes place in private.

The Court of Appeal in *R v Reakes* (1974) approved of the judge's direction on this matter when he said that the jury should decide whether the act was done in private by looking 'at all the surrounding circumstances, the time of night, the nature of the place including such matters as lighting and ... the likelihood of a third person coming upon the scene.' Private yards with public access, therefore, are unlikely to be private places at 1.00 am, as the jury appears to have thought in this case.

The only other guidance is to consider what the courts have understood to be public places when that question has arisen in other areas of the law (particularly in relation to public order). Care has to be taken with such guidance since it does not follow that because a place is not a public place that anything that happens there necessarily happens in private. In considering what is a public place, the courts have indicated that a place is a public place if the public, or a group of the public, have access to the place in fact, regardless of the legal right of the public to enter that place.

Therefore the question whether an act took place in private is very much a question of fact, the answer to which may conceivably vary from case to case. It would seem though that it is at least arguable that a private bedroom in accommodation such as a hostel or group home is a private place, provided no third persons (particularly members of staff) have ready, unannounced access to the room.

No offence is committed, as has been said, if both of the parties consent. As well as there being an age limit of 18 on this matter, there is also a restriction for people with severe learning difficulties. If either of the men suffers from 'severe mental handicap' (see section 2.5 for definition), he cannot, in law, consent to the act. A person, the defendant, will not be convicted of a homosexual act where the male victim is a man with severe mental handicap where the defendant 'did not know and had no reason to suspect that man to be suffering from severe mental handicap' (Sexual Offences Act 1967, s.1(3); see section 3.4 for the similar clause in the 1956 Act). This all appears to mean that:

i) two men both with severe mental handicap may legally have a homosexual relationship, if neither could be expected to, and do not, recognise the degree of impairment of his partner

ii) a man may have a homosexual relationship with a man with severe mental handicap if it could be argued that he did not know and had no reason to suspect that his partner has a severe mental handicap. This might particularly apply to a man with a mild learning difficulty.

Whilst homosexual relationships for men with learning difficulties are not legally straightforward these two points may be of some value in permitting non-exploitative relationships, especially when combined with the discretion to prosecute, which is unlikely to be exercised in favour of prosecution unless there is evidence of exploitation or abuse.

The above reflects the law as stated in the Sexual Offences Act 1967, s.1(3). However, confusion has arisen because of the way in which the Criminal Justice and Public Order Act 1994 amended the offence of buggery. The provisions now seem to state that buggery is not committed where the act is in private, between two consenting males, provided they are both 18. In so far as it goes, this merely restates the position under the 1967 Act. However, there is no mention of men with 'severe mental handicap'. So does the 1967 Act, s.1(3) apply or not? It is submitted that it does not (see also Card (1995)). Thus a man who has a 'severe mental handicap' may, in law, consent to what would otherwise be buggery provided he has the capacity to do so. There is no law saying he cannot consent.

If the understanding of the current law with regard to buggery is correct, there are fewer restrictions upon people with learning difficulties engaging in male homosexual acts than in heterosexual activity, lesbian acts, or two men engaging in gross indecency (which will usually apply to activity not involving the sexual act necessary for the offence of buggery). This is a surprising position, but appears to be the current law.

Where a prosecution discretion is to be exercised, it is submitted that the Crown Prosecution Service must take account of any exploitation or abuse and its absence is a factor militating against prosecution. The old Code for Crown Prosecutors provided advice which, it is submitted, is still valid, though it is not to be found in the current version of the Code:

'Whenever two or more persons have participated in the offence in circumstances rendering both or all liable to prosecution the Crown Prosecutor should take into account each person's age, the relative ages of the participants and whether or not there was any element of seduction or corruption when deciding whether, and if so in respect of whom, proceedings should be instituted.'

Despite the meaning of 'gross indecency' suggested above, gay couples kissing and cuddling in public may still be guilty of an offence. In *Masterson v Holden* (1986) a gay couple seen kissing and cuddling in Oxford Street by two heterosexual couples were guilty of an offence under s.5 of the Public Order Act 1936 of using 'insulting' behaviour whereby a breach of the peace was likely to happen. The behaviour was insulting because the display of such objectionable conduct in a public street 'may well be regarded by another person, particularly a young woman, as conduct which insults her by suggesting that she is somebody who would find such conduct in public acceptable herself.' The conduct was likely to result in a breach of the peace because the two male members of the heterosexual couples on hearing their girlfriends' comments hit the two gay men. Despite the repeal of the 1936 Act this would probably still be an offence under s.4 of the Public Order Act 1986, provided the approach in *Masterson v Holden* was thought to be valid.

The approach to the word 'insulting' adopted in *Masterson v Holden* appears to be stretching its meaning too far. Conduct may be offensive or objectionable but that does not make it insulting.

The court indicated that overt heterosexual conduct in public might also be insulting. It is difficult to believe that any heterosexual couple would ever find themselves in court charged with this offence after merely kissing and cuddling in public, and, if they were, even more difficult to believe that they would be found guilty.

Additional problems in sex education for people who are gay or lesbian are created by s.28 of the Local Government Act 1988 (see section 3.11).

3.11   Sex education and the law

Most forms of sex education will present no legal problems. This is because there is no specific offence covering the use of sex education material, apart from the obscenity laws which are of concern to the makers and suppliers.

Sex education is a part of the basic curriculum at both secondary and special schools, but all but the biological aspects of sex education have been taken out of the National Curriculum (see the Education Reform Act 1988, s.2(1) as amended by the Education Act 1993, s.241). For this purpose

'"Sex education" includes education about – (a) Acquired Immune Deficiency Syndrome and Human Immunodeficiency Virus, and (b) any other sexually transmitted disease' (Education Act 1944, s.114(1), as amended by the Education Act 1993, s.241).

Exemption from sex education may be sought by the parent of a pupil and that request will be granted, provided the pupil continues to be educated within the National Curriculum. Therefore a pupil may be exempt from all forms of sex education, except the biological aspects (Education Reform Act 1988, s.17A, as added by the Education Act 1993, s.241).

Sex education must still comply with the criteria laid down in the Education (No.2) Act 1986, which requires that the education authority, the governing body and the headteacher *'take such steps as are reasonably practicable to secure that where sex education is given to ... pupils ... it is given in such a manner as to encourage those pupils to have due regard to moral considerations and the value of family life.'*

Sex education, therefore, is an important part of a child's education. It is likely to be a part of a larger personal and social relationships programme.

If a local authority is involved in education, there is an additional problem in relation to dealing with homosexuality. Section 28 of the Local Government Act 1988 prohibits expenditure, except for the purpose of treating or preventing disease, for the promotion of homosexuality (see section 2.4). However, this does not appear to prevent expenditure on teaching about homosexuality at least on a need to know basis, for example, when a person is or may be homosexual in orientation or if a client needs to be educated so as to be able to deal appropriately with homosexual overtures whether or not they are or may be homosexual, since homosexuality is not being 'promoted'.

Sex education may, though, involve careful consideration of the following possibilities:

i)   Aiding and abetting another person's offence: as considered in section 3.4, it is a general principle of criminal law that a person can be guilty of a crime by causing or encouraging another to commit it or facilitating it or providing real assistance at the time the crime is committed. An example given in section 3.4 was of a member of staff assisting two people to have sexual intercourse.

If the staff activity is more remotely connected with an act of sexual intercourse, it is less likely that the member of staff has counselled or procured the offence itself. Since sex education is usually part of a wider social education programme it is unlikely that it has caused intercourse to take place.

Provision of contraceptive advice does not necessarily involve staff in the commission of an offence (see section 3.12), so also the provision of sex education is not likely to involve the commission of an offence, indeed is less likely to do so. It is important to emphasise the discretion to prosecute (see section 2.2).

Ultimately, as with many issues in this area, it is for staff to act in the best interests of their client. This is especially important when the law appears not to recognise the sexual needs in terms of education and activity of people with learning difficulties.

ii) Hands-on teaching methods: hands-on teaching of personal hygiene, such as toilet procedures and menstruation, needs to be considered albeit briefly. It .is highly unlikely that teaching such essential skills by a hands-on method when there was no alternative would be regarded as indecent (see section 3.9 on indecent assault), even if the client was a 'defective' and so in law could not consent.

Of much greater concern is the question of whether a member of staff may help a person with learning difficulties to (learn to) masturbate. This is one of the most difficult issues, legally and ethically. Consequently, the discussion centres of the question of teaching masturbation. The relevant offence is that of indecent assault on either a woman or a man under the Sexual Offences Act 1956 (see section 3.9; it is also the case that the offence of gross indecency may be relevant, see section 3.10).

Touching a man's penis or a woman's vagina would be an assault, technically a battery, because there is actual contact. Making the woman or man believe that they are about to be touched would also be an assault, technically this is the correct use of the word 'assault'. Consequently, if masturbation cannot be taught by relatively abstract methods, eg the showing of books, films, pictures, etc, the remaining teaching methods are likely to involve either a battery or an assault.

If the person being taught by such direct or hands-on methods is a 'defective' (see section 2.5) they cannot give legally valid consent, regardless of their actual capacity to consent or signs of willingness or desire to be so taught.

But, is the teaching of masturbation necessarily 'indecent'? The question is whether the acts (involving contact or not) would appear to the 'right-minded person' as being indecent in the sense that they are 'so offensive to contemporary standards of modesty and privacy' as to be regarded as indecent. If a jury or bench of magistrates would most likely be convinced that teaching personal hygiene skills is not indecent when done properly, so also it may be possible to convince them that teaching masturbation is not indecent.

Assistance in arguing this point would be provided by showing that the teaching took place in the context of a personal and social relationships programme that was tailored to the particular individual's needs; that they were being taught masturbation because they wanted it (if that can be ascertained) and that it was appropriate for them to have this skill. If there has been a full case conference at which agreement has been reached on a course of action involving a member of staff helping a client to masturbate, these points may well be more easily made. In *R v Hall* (1987) it is clear that the head teacher, on the most favourable interpretation, made the mistake of himself deciding to teach a girl how to masturbate, without any reference to anyone else involved in her care at all. Consequently, no sensible guidelines were followed. This case may also suggest that, at least for practical reasons, it may be well be inadvisable for a man to teach a woman. Further, the motivation of the member of staff would be relevant, so it would appear that if they have a decent motive this may well mean that what otherwise might appear to be an indecent act is in fact not (see section 3.9). Further, it also has to be shown against a defendant that they acted with an indecent intention. This may also permit the member of staff to show that they acted in a professionally appropriate manner and with a decent motive.

It is, of course, also the case that the only way such action will come to light is if it is reported. If the matter is reported, prosecution may well be unlikely, unless there is any evidence of exploitation (see section 2.2).

3.12 Medical treatment: under 16s

A person who is 16 or more years of age may provide consent to 'any surgical, medical or dental treatment' and that consent is 'as effective as it would be if he [or she] were of full age' (Family Law Reform Act 1969, s.8(1)). A person is of 'full age' at 18. This section clearly applies only to the person who is competent to make the particular treatment in question. The section does not deal with the validity of the consent of a person under the age of 16. *Gillick v Wisbech Area Health Authority* (1985) was concerned with this issue.

The *Gillick* case specifically concerned the provision of contraceptive advice and treatment to girls under 16 years of age, but it is also a general decision on consent to medical treatment by people under 16. Clearly, parental consent is essential sometimes, for example, when an operation is thought to be medically necessary for a baby. Even here parents do not have complete freedom of choice. Their decision is supposed to be taken in the best interests of the child. That a decision is taken in this way may be ensured through proceedings under the Children Act 1989 for a 'section 8 order' or through the wardship or inherent jurisdictions of the High Court. In these procedures the child's welfare is the paramount consideration. A court objectively decides whether a particular operation, or form of medical treatment, is in the best interests of the child. In general terms, the same approach will ... be taken whichever procedure is used (see, Lyon (1993) and Cretney and Masson (1990), Chapters 24, 25).

In *Gillick*, the House of Lords indicated that people under 16 can consent to some forms of medical treatment. Lord Scarman said that 'the parental right to determine whether or not a minor child below the age of 16 will have medical treatment terminates if and when the child achieves a sufficient understanding and intelligence to enable him or her to understand fully what is proposed. It will be a question of fact whether a child seeking advice has sufficient understanding of what is involved to give a consent valid in law.' In short, a person under 16 may consent (subject to certain limitations considered below) to treatment if they have sufficient understanding and intelligence (see Lyon (1993), pp 61-62).

The *Gillick* case was primarily concerned with the provision of contraceptive advice and treatment to girls under the age of 16. The additional problem with this form of treatment is that it is an offence for a man to have unlawful sexual intercourse with a girl under 16 (see section 3.3). So, it appeared that a doctor (or other person) providing the contraceptive advice and treatment to the girl would be aiding and abetting the man in committing this offence. Nevertheless, a majority of the House of Lords felt that the existing Government guidance was lawful when it indicated that girls could be provided with contraceptive advice and treatment without their parents being informed. However, doctors cannot simply provide such advice and treatment if they have the girl's consent: certain conditions have to be fulfilled. Lord Fraser stated these conditions as follows:

'The doctor will... be justified in proceeding without the parents' consent or even knowledge provided he is satisfied on the following matters: (1) that the girls (although under 16 years of age) will understand his advice; (2) that he cannot persuade her to inform her parents or to allow him to inform the parents that she is seeking contraceptive advice; (3) that she is very likely to begin or to continue having sexual intercourse with or without contraceptive treatment; (4) that unless she receives contraceptive advice or treatment her physical or mental health or both are likely to suffer; (5) that her best interests require him to give her contraceptive advice, treatment or both without the parental consent.'

Despite the apparent breadth of the decision in *Gillick*, it is clear that there are certain limits upon the decision-making of a person under 16. First, it may turn out that there are certain forms of highly intrusive treatment that the courts eventually decide no 15 year old, let alone someone younger, could possibly ever have sufficient understanding or intelligence to provide consent. However, in *Re P (a minor)* (1986) it was decided that a schoolgirl aged 15 could have an abortion, which is a major treatment, despite her parents' objection.

Secondly, the child under 16 may provide consent, but this does not mean that they can prevent the treatment being provided. The Court of Appeal in *Re W (a minor) (medical treatment)* (1992) decided that consent could be sought, potentially, from one of three sources: the child; a parent (or someone with parental responsibility, see Lyon (1993), pp 68-73); the court. Any could provide consent. Indeed a parent or the court could consent, even where the child was refusing consent. The decision was actually concerned with a child over 16, but it is clear that, whilst a child under 16 may provide consent, they may not refuse consent. Thirdly, the child must be competent to make the decision. In *Re R (a minor) (wardship: consent to treatment)* (1992), the Court of Appeal decided that where a child's competency fluctuated because of a mental disorder, this meant that she was not competent to make a decision, even if she happened to be in a 'lucid period'. It is understood that neither of these two latter cases apply to adults; and that the decisions, whilst appearing particularly strange, are predicated on the need to protect young people and children.

The position is the same whether or not the girl or boy has learning difficulties. The direct relevance of the *Gillick* case is to girls with learning difficulties who are under 16 years of age. Indirectly, the case may have something to say about competence generally, although there are now cases particularly concerned with this issue (see section 3.14).

3.12A	**Medical treatment: people under 18**

The Family Law Reform Act 1969, s.8 provides that the consent of a person who is 16 is as effective as that of someone of full age (see also section 3.12). Therefore, provided the person is competent to make the decision, their decision is valid and authorises the treatment. However, it is important to note, first, that if the competency of such a person fluctuates, they are to be regarded as incompetent, even though they might be factually competent at the time (*Re R (a minor) (wardship: medical treatment)* (1992)). It is assumed that this decision applies to people who are 16 but under 18, although it concerned a 15 year old girl. This rule does not apply to adults. Secondly, a person who is between 16 and 18 has no right effectively to refuse treatment. The treatment provider can look to either a parent (or someone with parental responsibility) or the court to provide the necessary consent. This follows from the decision of the Court of Appeal in *Re W (a minor) (medical treatment)* (1992) which concerned a 16 year old girl.

3.13 Medical treatment: people under 18 who cannot consent

In the case of a person under the age of 18 who cannot consent, the consent of a parent (or someone with parental responsibility) to treatment is, at least initially, essential. Although parents have the responsibility to take such decisions, they do not have unbridled decision-making power. If there is any disagreement about the parental decision (for example between professionals and parents), a 'section 8 order' could be sought under the Children Act 1989 or the child might be made a ward of court or the court might be asked to exercise its inherent jurisdiction to make the treatment decision. Whatever procedure is used, the same basic principles apply (there are differences, but these are not considered for present purposes). Indeed, the wardship cases would appear to be good guidance not only as to future wardship cases and exercises of the court's inherent jurisdiction, but also as pointers to decisions under the Children Act 1989. Section 8 orders will largely supplant wardship and the exercise of the inherent jurisdiction.

One instructive wardship cases concerned a 12 year old girl who was suffering from Sotos' Syndrome. Her mother and doctor wanted the girl to be sterilised. The court did not agree that a sterilisation operation was appropriate in the circumstances. It was pointed out that the girl was young and not sexually active. Her development might be such that she would be able to deal with her sexuality without such intrusive methods when she was older. She might in the future understand the consequences of sterilisation and then she might wish to marry. If the operation were carried out it could have long-term psychological effects *(Re D (a minor)* (1976)).

Given different facts, the courts may reach a different conclusion. In *Re B* (1987) (otherwise known as 'the Jeanette case'), the House of Lords was convinced that the circumstances of the girl in question were so different from those of the girl in *Re D* that the courts should authorise a sterilisation operation under the wardship jurisdiction.

It is to be stressed that the House of Lords underlined the statement that had been made in *Re D* that the woman's right to reproduce was a basic human right. No woman should be deprived of that right lightly. *Re B* does not overrule *Re D*. Indeed this principle has been reiterated in the context of adults in *Re F* (see section 3.14).

Further, the House of Lords made it clear in *Re B* that sterilisations could not be carried out for eugenic purposes. Neither can they be carried out for social purposes. Thus sterilisations cannot be performed when the objective is simply to make the person more easily manageable.

The facts of *Re B* were very different from those in *Re D*. This goes some way to explaining why a different decision was reached. Some people take the view that sterilisations should never be carried out on women who have learning difficulties or at least not when the sterilisation is for non-therapeutic purposes (this is also the view of the Supreme Court of Canada in *Re Eve* (1986)). The House in *Re B* did not accept these viewpoints, rather it accepted that in some circumstances it may be in the best interests of the child/ward/person under 1 that she be sterilised.

Each case depends upon its own facts, and so care should be taken in assuming that the same decision will be made by the courts even when the facts appear to be strikingly similar. Nevertheless, it is instructive to consider *Re B* in a bit more detail.

Jeanette is described in the law reports as having 'a "moderat degree of mental handicap', with limited intellectual development. Her ability to understand speech was that of a 'six year old child' and her ability to express herself was that of a 'two year old child'. She was capable of certain tasks, including coping with menstruation. However, it was said that she would never be able to care for herself in the community, nor would she be able to return full time to her mother's care. She was 'unlikely to show an improvement in mental capacity beyond that of a six year old child'. She had been living in a residential institution from the age of four. She suffered from epilepsy, for which she was at the time receiving the anti-convulsant drug, sodium valproate. She had in the past shown evidence of extremes of mood and had been violent and aggressive. This was associated with pre-menstrual tension, for which she received the drug, danazol, which also helped to control her irregular periods. Further she suffered from obesity. This limited the range of drugs which she could be offered. Indeed when receiving Microgynon 30, an oral contraceptive used to treat her outbursts of violence, it was found that her weight increased significantly. Finally she had a high tolerance to pain, indeed would open her own wounds.

It was indicated that she was becoming sexually aware, which was shown through advances to male members of staff and 'touching herself in the genital area.' It was felt that there was an obvious risk of pregnancy. This was to be avoided, because she had no maternal feelings, and was not capable of bringing up any child to which she gave birth, although, if a child had to be taken away it would not cause her distress'. She understood the link between pregnancy and child birth, but not the link between sexual intercourse and pregnancy and it was not possible to teach her 'about sexuality in any abstract form'. She was incapable of making an informed choice about contraception. If she became pregnant, termination would be desirable. Because of her obesity, the fact that she was pregnant might not be discovered until termination was impossible. Although she would probably be able to cope with the pregnancy, the delivery would be traumatic, requiring a Caesarean section, the scars of which she would not allow to heal.

On these grounds, it was felt that 'effective contraception' measures had to be taken in the best interests of the girl herself. Many options apparently were canvassed in the medical evidence supplied to the court. The House of Lords mentioned four. The first was to keep her away from men. This, of course, was not possible in the light of the current philosophy of care for people with learning difficulties. The second was mechanical methods which were rejected because of her 'limited intellectual capacity'. The third was provision of the drug progestogen in pill form. The fourth was sterilisation by occluding the fallopian tubes, which was to be regarded as irreversible.

The House compared the latter two and came down in favour of sterilisation, because it was 'a relatively minor operation carrying a small degree of risk to the patient, a very high degree of protection and minimal side-effects'. On the other hand the use of the drug did not appear to be so acceptable for four reasons.

First, it would have to continue, uninterruptedly for a considerable period of time (about 30 years). Secondly, it had to be given in daily dosage which might not always be possible because of the girl's proneness to aggression and violence when it was quite possible that no-one would be able to give her the drug. Thirdly, the side effects of the drug over the period of time in question were unknown. Finally, the effectiveness of this option was entirely speculative. No trial was possible, because the girl was very nearly 18 at which age the court could no longer take a decision on contraceptive treatment under its warship jurisdiction. The court felt that the decision had to be taken at the time.

A critique of this decision is fairly obvious, particularly since there have been some important legal changes. First, decisions can be made once a person is 18, so there is now no need to make permanent decisions before that age; secondly, the assessment of the risks and benefits and of the number of options is limited; thirdly, there is not always an upper time limit upon terminations of pregnancy (see section 3.14); and finally, the decision fails to give primacy to the need to regard a person with learning difficulties as no different from anyone else as much as possible.

The decision does not mean that other girls will be sterilised. It gives an indication of the circumstances in which a sterilisation operation might be authorised in future.

3.14 Medical treatment for adults: sterilisation and abortion

i) Capacity to decide

The starting point in considering any form of medical treatment, including sterilisation and abortion, is that no operation may be performed on an adult without her or his consent. The consent of a person to surgical, medical or dental treatment is usually valid from the age of 16 (Family Law Reform Act 1969, s.8; and see section 3.12A) and may be valid under that age if the person has sufficient understanding and intelligence (see section 3.12).

In *Re C* (1993), the most recent decision on testing the capacity of adults to make treatment decisions, the judge thought that the question for consideration was whether 'Mr. C's capacity is so reduced by his chronic mental illness that he does not sufficiently understand the nature, purpose and effects of the proffered amputation.' An expert witness had identified a three-stage process which the judge thought helpful:

i) 'comprehending and retaining treatment information'

ii) 'believing it', and

iii) 'weighing it in the balance to arrive at choice'.

This sets a slightly different, and probably higher, test than the requirement that the individual must understand in broad terms the proposed treatment, as propounded by the judge in *Chatterton v Gerson* (1981). There is also the guidance to be found in the Mental Health Act Code of Practice (1993) which provides, at paragraph 15.10:

'An individual in order to have capacity must be able to:

– understand what medical treatment is and that somebody has proposed that he needs it and why the treatment is being proposed;

– understand in broad terms the nature of the proposed treatment;

– understand its principal benefits and risks;

– understand what will be the consequences of not receiving the proposed treatment;

– possess the capacity to make a choice.'

The lack of certainty as to which test to follow is unfortunate. Perhaps the best advice is that the decision in *Re C* should be followed, being the most recent authoritative statement (see Gunn (1994)). Capacity is identified in relation to a particular decision at a particular time, and not generally. Refusal of treatment does not make the person incompetent.

In addition to satisfying the test for capacity, a person must not be under pressure to arrive at a particular answer. Undue influence will invalidate an apparent consent (*Re T (adult: refusal of medical treatment)* (1992)).

ii)   Information provision
Further, the law requires that an individual be given a certain amount of information before consent is given, even if they do not ask any questions about the proposed treatment. A case in the House of Lords has established that the doctor need not give her/his patient all the relevant information before seeking consent. The majority of the judges took the view that the doctors must give the amount of information that is consonant with a responsible body of medical opinion (*Sidaway* (1985)).

iii) Exceptions to the general rule: the Mental Health Act 1983
The preceding principles apply to all people and all proposed forms of treatment unless exceptions are made by either statute or case law. The Mental Health Act 1983 creates such an

exception. The treatment provisions of the Act, to be found in Part IV, sections 56-64, apply only to certain detained patients (that is people relatively long-term detained, ie mainly under ss.2 or 3, and some of the admissions through the criminal justice system) and concern only medical treatment provided for the mental disorder from which the patient is suffering. (Note in passing that the protections of the Act additional to the need for the patient's consent with regard to psychosurgery and the surgical implantation of hormones to reduce male sexual drive apply also to informal patients.)

The Court of Appeal in *B v Croydon H.A.* (1995) has provided an extended application of the Mental Health Act 1983. Where a person is a detained patient, treatment (other than psychosurgery, the surgical implantation of hormones to reduce male sexual drive, electro-convulsive therapy, and the continuation of medication for mental disorder after the first three months of its administration) which is for the mental disorder from which the patient is suffering may be given without the patient's consent (Mental Health Act 1983, s.63). The Court of Appeal interpreted this provision to mean that treatments which are ancillary to a core treatment are covered by s.63 and so may be given without consent. In the case itself, the patient was suffering from a psychopathic disorder and the core treatment she was receiving was psychotherapeutic psychoanalysis (which is clearly a treatment for mental disorder) and the ancillary treatment was force feeding through a naso-gastric tube when she starved herself. It is not easy to see how this is treatment for the mental disorder from which B was suffering. It appears that treatment will be ancillary where it is:

'Nursing and care concurrent with the core treatment or as a necessary prerequisite to such treatment or to prevent the patient from causing harm to himself or to alleviate the consequences of the disorder ...' (*B v Croydon H.A.* (1994), p 687)

There is an element of discretion in determining whether a treatment is so ancillary and thus falls under the Mental Health Act. This approach clearly extends the Act considerably and, it is submitted, is an improper extension (see Gunn (1995)). It is asserted that sterilisation and abortion would never be sufficiently ancillary and so would continue to fall outside the Mental Health Act 1983.

It continues to be the case that the treatments definitely covered by the Mental Health Act 1983 s.63 include behaviour modification.

iv) Treatment where the adult is incapable of deciding

The House of Lords had to consider the question of whether an adult woman with learning difficulties who could not consent could be sterilised in *Re F* (1990) (see, Morgan (1990), Gunn (1990), Shaw (1990)). This case also sets the criteria for treating adults who cannot consent, whatever the treatment that is proposed (unless it falls within the Mental Health Act 1983).

It is essential to stress that the first requirement is that the particular woman in question cannot consent to the treatment in question at the time the treatment is proposed and carried out. If they are competent, they must be allowed to make the decision.

It is only if they are determined to be not competent of deciding that *Re F* becomes relevant, since, as Lord Goff said, 'the fundamental principle, now long established [is] that every person's body is inviolate.'

The solution provided by the House of Lords in *Re F* demands consideration of three issues once it has been determined that the person for whom the treatment is proposed is not competent to consent to that treatment:

i) Treatment can be provided when the action taken is to preserve life, health or well-being. Consequently, the forms of action involved are not limited either to those which are therapeutic, since 'well-being' clearly includes actions not designed to deal with a health problem and consequently non-therapeutic sterilisation is permitted. Nor must the treatment be 'serious', since it is clearly anticipated that this approach can apply to what might be termed 'routine treatment'.

ii) If the action is for the incompetent person's life, health or well-being, the doctor may only act in the 'best interests' of that person. It is anticipated that in the already mentioned 'routine treatment' cases, this requirement will cause little difficulty, although this assumption may be open to question in, eg dental treatment. In order to be acting in the person's best interests whether it be routine or other forms of treatment, the doctor (or other health care provider) must 'act in accordance with a responsible and competent body of relevant professional opinion'. There is an expectation that the treatment provider will consult with specialists, a multi-disciplinary team where (as it is submitted is usually the case) the decision is not a purely medical one, relatives and others who are concerned with the care of the patient.

iii) There is no requirement that the opinion of a court be obtained to assist in the determination of the question whether a particular course of action is in the incompetent person's best interests. It is expected, however, that in some cases, the treatment provider would wish to seek the guidance of the court as to whether or nor a particular form of treatment is in the person's best interests, by way of seeking a declaration whereby the court will state whether, in its view, such is the case or not. Consequently, the House of Lords expects that the court will be able to provide 'an independent, objective and authoritative view on the lawfulness of the procedure in the particular circumstances of the ... case ...'

v)   Sterilisation

The House of Lords in *Re F* expected that such declarations would, as a matter of practice, be obtained when the action proposed was sterilisation. It is suggested that this is of particular importance since the question of whether such an operation is in the best interests of the patient is not a purely medical matter, if any treatment decision may be described as such. The issues which were identified indicating that such treatment ought not to be carried out without seeking a declaration were:

– it is a basic human right of a woman to reproduce

– '... there is a fear that those responsible for mental patients might (perhaps unwittingly) seek them to be sterilised as a matter of administrative convenience.'

–   the operation is (usually) irreversible.

On the facts of the case a declaration was provided which authorised the sterilisation of F.

Since that decision, the Official Solicitor has issued guidance which should be followed when a declaration is being sought to sterilise someone who is not competent to make the decision themselves. Technical information as to the method whereby a court's view of the appropriateness of a proposal for sterilisation may be obtained is provided. It indicates the importance of seeking the views of a court and expects that in most, if not all, cases there will be a hearing with the person upon whom the operation is to be carried out being independently represented by the Official Solicitor. The purpose of the process is identified as being 'to establish whether or not the proposed sterilisation is in the best interests of the patient. The judge will require to be satisfied that those proposing sterilisation are seeking it in good faith and that their paramount concern is for the best interests of the patient rather than their own or the public's convenience. The proceedings will normally involve a thorough adversarial investigation of all possible viewpoints and any possible alternatives to sterilisation. Nevertheless, straightforward cases proceeding without dissent may be disposed of at the hearing for directions without oral evidence.' It is suggested that the identification of 'straightforward cases' should be rare, unless by this is meant those cases in which there is a clear and present health care need for the operation, such as ovarian cancer.

It is anticipated that 'the judge will expect to receive comprehensive medical, psychological and social evaluations of the patient from appropriately qualified experts.' The Official Solicitor anticipates that the judge will require evidence clearly establishing:

i)   that the 'patient' cannot make their own decision and 'is unlikely to develop sufficiently to make an informed judgment about sterilisation in the foreseeable future. In this connection it must be borne in mind:

– that the fact that a person is legally incompetent for some purposes does not mean that he or she necessarily lacks the capacity to make a decision about sterilisation and

– that in the case of a minor his or her youth and potential for development may make it difficult or impossible to make the relevant finding of incapacity.

ii) that there is a real need for contraception because the 'patient' is 'physically capable of procreation' and 'is likely to engage in sexual activity, at the present or in the near future, under circumstances where there is a real danger as opposed to mere chance that pregnancy is likely to result.'

iii) 'that the patient will experience substantial trauma or psychological damage if the condition which it is sought to avoid should arise, eg in the case of a contraceptive sterilisation that:

– the patient (if a woman) is likely if she becomes pregnant or gives birth to experience substantial trauma or psychological damage greater than that resulting from the sterilisation itself and

– the patient is permanently incapable of caring for a child even with reasonable assistance, eg from a future spouse in a case where the patient has or may have the capacity to marry.'

iv) 'that there is no practicable less intrusive alternative means of solving the anticipated problem than immediate sterilisation, in other words that:

– sterilisation is advisable at the time of the application rather than in the future;

– the proposed method of sterilisation entails the least invasion of the patient's body;

– sterilisation will not itself cause physical or psychological damage greater than the intended beneficial effects;

–   the current state of scientific and medical knowledge does not suggest either that a reversible sterilisation procedure or other less drastic solutions to the problem sought to be avoided, eg, some other contraceptive method, will shortly be available or that science is on the threshold of an advance in the treatment of the patient's disability; and

–   in the case of a contraceptive sterilisation all less drastic contraceptive methods, including supervision, education and training, have proved unworkable or inapplicable.' (Practice Note (Official Solicitor: Sterilisation) 1990).

vi) Abortion

If it is proposed that a pregnancy be terminated the woman's consent must be obtained or the termination authorised under the law established by the House of Lords in *Re F* (1990). It will be surprising that a declaration need not be sought where the woman is not competent to decide, provided that the criteria in the Abortion Act 1967 are satisfied (*Re SG* (1990)). It is suggested that criteria other than those within the Abortion Act should be considered and that this ought to be done through seeking a declaration.

Termination of pregnancy is a criminal offence contrary to the Offences Against the Person Act 1861. It is only lawful if it is performed within the requirements of the Abortion Act 1967, as amended by s.37 of the Human Fertilisation and Embryology Act 1990. The Abortion Act requires that two doctors agree that in their opinions, made in good faith, at least one of the criteria permitting termination is present.

The 1967 Act, as amended, indicates that the following are the only criteria permitting lawful abortions:

i)   that the pregnancy has not exceeded its twenty-fourth week and that the continuance of the pregnancy would involve risk, greater than if the pregnancy were terminated, of injury to the physical or mental health of the pregnant woman or any existing children of her family; or *ii)* that the termination is necessary to prevent grave permanent injury to the physical or mental health of the pregnant woman; or

iii) that the continuance of the pregnancy would involve risk to the life of the pregnant woman greater than if the pregnancy were terminated; or

iv) that there is a substantial risk that if the child were born it would suffer from such physical or mental abnormalities as to be seriously handicapped.

The woman's actual or foreseeable environment can only be taken into account in assessing the risk of injury to health referred to in the first two criteria above. Bad environment does not in itself permit termination.

There is an upper time limit only for terminations under criterion *i)*.

vii) The future: reform?

The Law Commission has proposed that a Mental Incapacity Bill be introduced to provide a proper framework for decisions about many things, including medical treatment, where the adult in question is not capable of making that decision (Law Commission (1995); see Gunn (1995)). The Lord Chancellor is to conduct a consultation exercise on the proposals and the outcome of that process will assist in determining whether change along the lines proposed by the Law Commission will happen.

Sexual abuse of adults with learning difficulties

4.1 Introduction

Child abuse, and particularly child sexual abuse, has been much discussed recently. It has given rise to a considerable literature which may well be of assistance even where the victim is an adult (see the 'References' section in Spencer & Flin (1993)). Increasing concern has also been expressed about the possibility of abuse, particularly sexual abuse, of vulnerable adults. In recent years there have been more and more disclosures by adults with learning difficulties of instances of sexual abuse. Valuable information may be available from the analogous area of child sexual abuse. But since the victim is an adult and not a child, different responses are required. In particular, the legal methods of responding to child sexual abuse cannot simply be transferred to responding to the abuse of adults with learning difficulties. Much, but not all, of the legal response when the victim is a child is on the basis of child care law which, of course, does not apply to adults.

4.2 The general legal approach

The law may deal with instances of abuse by seeking to prosecute, and find guilty, the abusers. This will require the involvement of the victim. If the victim cannot or will not be involved, for whatever reason, then seeking to deal with abuse through criminal (and perhaps civil procedures) may not be possible. Alternative methods of responding to the abuse have to be sought, and these may well involve action taken with regard to the victim rather than the abuser, as is the case, for example, when care proceedings are taken with regard to the victim of child sexual abuse. The possible criminal proceedings are considered (see sections 4.3, 4.4, 4.5, 4.6, 4.7). The methods of dealing with abuse by civil methods are not considered further, although they may have significant advantages over criminal proceedings, particularly since the burden of proof on the victim is not as great as the burden of proof in criminal proceedings on the prosecution (the Crown Prosecution Service). Even so there may still be significant evidential problems in establishing that the defendant (the alleged abuser) did abuse the plaintiff. Success in civil proceedings means that the plaintiff receives damages (compensation for injury in money). The significant factor to be weighed against damages is that the plaintiff must pay the costs of the case, unless (as may well be the case) they receive financial support for an action through the legal aid system. There is no question of the victim paying for criminal proceedings. For further consideration of the legal methods of dealing with abuse, including the civil law, see Gunn (1989).

The possible alternative methods of dealing with abuse by the law are looked at in section 4.8.

4.3 Criminal offences and the sexual abuse of adults with learning difficulties

The usual method considered first to deal with the sexual abuse of adults with learning difficulties is whether any criminal offences have been committed against the victim. There are a number of criminal offences which appear to be well suited to dealing with sexual abuse. The main group of offences is that which might be headed 'sexual offences', although other offences against the person may also have a role to play. Further there is one offence which specifically deals with the neglect and ill-treatment of 'mentally disordered' people, that is s.127 of the Mental Health Act 1983 (section 4.6).

4.4 Sexual offences

The sexual offences which might deal with abuse are many of those already considered, albeit from a different perspective. The offences which will be considered when there is a disclosure of sexual abuse include:

— **rape**, which is committed where a man has sexual intercourse (whether vaginal or anal) with a woman or a man who does not consent, and he either knows that they do not consent to it or is reckless as to whether they consent to it or not (Sexual Offences Act 1956, s.1, as amended by the Criminal Justice and Public Order Act 1994). The woman or man does not have to be forced; they must simply not consent to sexual intercourse (see Smith & Hogan, (1992) and *R v Olugboja* (1981)). This offence may apply to a woman or a man with learning difficulties, since she or he may refuse her or his consent and simply submitting to the wishes of the man is not the same as consent. Thus whether or not they are a defective should not prevent consideration of this offence as a response to sexual abuse (see also sections 3.2, 3.4).

— **unlawful sexual intercourse with girls under 13 and under 16**, offences which have been considered above at section 3.3.

— **indecent assault**, which is committed where a person assaults another person indecently without that other's consent (a full consideration of these requirements is undertaken at section 3.9). This offence covers a man sexually abusing a woman without having intercourse with her and also covers a man abusing another man (in addition to the homosexual offences, see below) and a woman abusing either a man or another woman.

— **buggery**, which is committed by a man having anal intercourse with another man or a woman, and by a man or a woman having sex with an animal.

— **incest**, the one offence which deals specifically with a woman committing an offence when having sex with a man, all other instances have to be considered within the offence of indecent assault. A woman commits incest if she is at least 16 and permits 'a man whom she knows to be her grandfather, father, brother or son to have sexual intercourse with her by her consent' (s. 11(1) of the Sexual Offences Act 1956). A man commits incest if he has 'sexual intercourse with a woman he knows to be his granddaughter, daughter, sister or mother'

(s. 10(1) of the Sexual Offences Act 1956). It will be noticed that the offence of incest is limited to close relations, which are different where the offender is a woman as compared to when the offender is a man.

– **homosexual offences**. There are only specific offences where men are concerned; female homosexuality is dealt with by the offence of indecent assault. The various specific offences have been considered at section 3.10. In addition to these offences which are of general application, there are a number of crimes which mean that it is illegal to have sexual intercourse with, or otherwise have or encourage sexual relationships with, a person who is a 'defective' (for the meaning of this word, see section 2.5):

– **unlawful sexual intercourse with a woman who is a defective.** This offence has been considered at section 3.4. It must be stressed that it is committed whether or not the woman consents. Thus any element of exploitation of a woman who is a 'defective' may be responded to by the law, even if the man manages to obtain the woman's consent, without committing rape.

– **procurement of a woman who is a defective.** It is an offence, contrary to s. 9 of the Sexual Offences Act 1956, 'for a person to procure a woman who is a defective to have unlawful sexual intercourse in any part of the world.' Procure requires that the offender has encouraged the woman to have sexual intercourse. As with the previous offence, it is not an offence if the alleged offender did not know and had no reason to suspect that the woman was a defective.

– **permitting use of premises for sexual intercourse with a woman who is a defective**. This offence has been considered at section 3.5, but clearly performs an important-role in dealing with sexual abuse since, as with the previous offence, it involves an organiser, encourager or facilitator in an offence. In addition, such people might, of course, be aiding and abetting a man to commit the offence of having unlawful sexual intercourse with a woman who is a defective (see sections 3.4, 3.11).

—   **male staff having sex with female or male 'patients'.** This offence also considered above, see section 3.6, is clearly concerned to deal with abuse.

—   **taking a woman who is a defective away from the care of her parent with the purpose that she shall have unlawful sexual intercourse with a man**, see section 3.4.

This is an apparently comprehensive list of offences outlawing non-consensual sexual activity and also sexual activity with people who might be regarded as vulnerable. It is at this point that a dilemma has to be recognised. These offences are primarily concerned to prevent sexual abuse and exploitation, but the last group of offences also has the effect of restricting, if not prohibiting in some circumstances, appropriate sexual relationships for adults who are described as 'defective', although it has no restrictions for most adults with learning difficulties. A proper balance needs to be maintained between these ideals. Currently this balance is not maintained by the words of the law, but by the way it is applied through staff and parents dealing sensibly and sensitively with issues of sexuality and the police and Crown Prosecution Service responding in like fashion.

4.5	**Other offences against the person**

In addition to the sexual offences, there are a range of other offences against the person which may be of relevance. The least serious offence against the person is that consisting of either or both a common assault or a battery. These two concepts are classically defined as follows:

i)   an assault is any act by which the actor, intentionally or recklessly, causes the victim to apprehend immediate and unlawful personal violence;

ii)   a battery is any act by which the actor, intentionally or recklessly, inflicts unlawful personal violence upon the victim.

Consequently, any actual or apprehended contact (which is all that is required for 'violence') is a criminal offence, provided at least that the risk of that contact occurring is recognised by the actor. It is also an offence to assault someone occasioning them actual bodily harm (which is relatively minor harm).

As regards offences resulting in the causing of greater harm, it is usually not necessary to establish that the victim was assaulted or battered, but merely that they caused harm to the victim. Thus there are offences concerned with the inflicting and causing of grievous bodily harm, which is otherwise described as serious bodily harm and may vary upwards from something like a broken nose.

If death is caused a person may be liable for either murder or manslaughter. The difference between these offences lies in the purpose with which they act. A person is guilty of murder if they intend to kill or cause grievous bodily harm. A person is guilty of manslaughter if in the course of committing some other crime they kill the victim or if they cause the death of the victim, being grossly negligent as to the risk of death.

Finally, it is also an offence falsely (without lawful justification) to imprison another (that is, unreasonably restrict their movement). (As to all these offences see Smith & Hogan (1992)).

4.6   Ill-treatment and neglect of 'mentally disordered' people

S.127 of the Mental Health Act 1983 creates an offence which appears to deal directly with at least some forms of abuse, including sexual abuse:

'(**1**) *It shall be an offence for any person who is an officer on the staff or otherwise employed in, or who is one of the managers of, a hospital or mental nursing home -*

(**a**) *to ill-treat or wilfully to neglect a patient for the time being receiving treatment for mental disorder as an in-patient in that hospital or home; or*

(**b**) *to ill-treat or wilfully to neglect, on the premises on which the hospital or home forms part, a patient for the time being receiving such treatment there as an out-patient.'*

This offence, whilst being of considerable importance, only applies to what happens within hospitals or mental nursing homes. Consequently, s.127(2) is likely to be of more significance:

'(**2**) *It shall be an offence for any individual to ill-treat or wilfully to neglect a mentally disordered patient who is for the time being subject to his guardianship under this Act or otherwise in his custody or care (whether by virtue of any legal or moral obligation or otherwise).*'

R v Newington (1990) has provided much needed guidance as to the meaning of this offence, which is concerned with people living in the community, including people who live in residential care homes and other accommodation whether or not it has to be registered under the Registered Homes Act 1984 or other legislation. The case is concerned with the 'ill-treatment' form of the offence, rather than 'neglect' although some of the points are of general application.

The guidance the case provides is important in the following respects:

i)   It is now clear that ill-treatment may have occurred where no injury is caused to the victim. The offence deals with a wide range of conduct including the conditions in which residents in homes live and, possibly, the use of harsh words and gratuitous bullying.

ii)   It is not necessarily the case that the use of 'violence' will amount to ill-treatment. 'Violence' may be justifiable in self-defence, for the prevention of crime, to treat people who cannot consent for themselves or, according to this case, 'for the reasonable control of a patient'. It is not clear on what basis force used in the last set of circumstances would be justifiable, unless this is another example of the use of the defence of necessity.

iii)   The victim of the ill-treatment or wilful neglect must be a 'mentally disordered patient'. This phrase simply means that the person be someone who is suffering or appearing to be suffering from a mental disorder (see section 2.5). The word 'patient' simply means 'person' in this context. However, they must also, as s. 127 states, be either in the guardianship under the Mental Health Act 1983 of the defendant or otherwise under their care and control, whether as a consequence of a legal or moral obligation.

iv)   The conduct amounting to ill-treatment must be done deliberately and there must be an appreciation by the defendant at the time either that they were inexcusably ill-treating a patient or that she was reckless as to whether she was inexcusably acting in that way.

4.7   Problems with the law

In the context of sexual offences, it has already been pointed out that a difficult balance has to be drawn between the function of the law to prevent abuse and exploitation and the need of people with learning difficulties to be able to express themselves sexually in an appropriate fashion.

It may appear that the brief reference to a range of criminal offences suggests that there are numerous methods which can be used to deal with the sexual abuse of vulnerable people with learning difficulties. However, there are a considerable number of problems:

i)   The legal response involves a reaction after the abuse has happened. There is otherwise nothing upon which legal action can be based. It is contrary to the rule of law to act against a person merely upon suspicion. It is, therefore, accurate to describe the approach of the law through prosecuting for a criminal offence as reactive only. The only way the law can prevent abuse is in the hope that either its mere existence stops people acting contrary to law or it reflects morality which stops people abusing others.

ii)   The law also may have a preventive function, in that it permits 'self-help' that is, primarily, a person acting in self-defence to ward off an attack. This demands proper education directed at the appropriateness of saying 'no' for people with learning difficulties, for whom it may be particularly difficult to act with such confidence and assertiveness.

iii) The criminal law option is not usually available unless first the police and later the Crown Prosecution Service are involved (private prosecutions are possible, although these are highly unlikely in the circumstances, if for no other reason than that there is no financial assistance available for someone who wishes to institute such a prosecution). This is likely to involve either the victim or someone on his/her behalf reporting the matter. Perhaps the most traumatic part of this process will be the need to undergo a number of interviews to provide the investigating and prosecuting authorities with knowledge as to what happened and to determine whether they believe a case is established such that further investigation and ultimately prosecution is appropriate. Such interviews may be extremely difficult because the abuse incident(s) has to be relived and the victim may well feel that it is s/he who is on trial.

iv) There may well be special problems if it is decided that the case should go to court as a prosecution of the alleged abuser. These problems (which will also affect civil actions) lie with the need to give evidence upon which it would be possible to found a conviction. The nature of much sexual abuse is that the victim may be the only person who can give evidence against the abuser. If that is the case, a person with learning difficulties may face first someone raising the question whether they are capable of taking the oath and, therefore, being competent to give evidence. No particularly stringent test is applied. It is to be determined whether the person understands that the oath taken before giving evidence is a solemn promise to tell the truth, involving more than the ordinary duty to tell the truth in daily life, and that they appreciate the seriousness of the occasion. It is not necessary to establish the extent of a witness's belief in God and therefore of the divine sanction (*R v Bellamy* (1985), and see Keane (1989)). The question is to be determined in open court in the absence of the jury, and expert evidence is admissible to assist in determining whether a person with learning difficulties is competent to take the oath (*R v Hampshire* (1995); *R v Deakin* (1994).

Secondly, the witness with learning difficulties must be able to present their story in a believable fashion, without the aid of leading questions from the prosecuting lawyer. Thus they must be able to present their story without any guidance other than fairly bland questions which do not suggest a particular answer or remind the witness of what the answer should be. Expert evidence is not admissible for the prosecution so as to promote the reliability or credibility of the witness. If the defence attacks the credibility or reliability of the witness on the basis of, eg learning disability and this matter is outside the experience of the jury, it is possible that expert evidence in rebuttal may be used (*R v Robinson* (1994)).

Thirdly, that witness having presented their story must then be able to withstand the pressure of cross-examination, where it is the function of the lawyer for the defence to ascertain whether there are any inconsistencies or inaccuracies in the story. These last two problems may be termed as a consideration of whether the person with learning difficulties will 'come up to proof'. One means of amelioration of the trauma of giving evidence, especially in a sexual abuse case, is the possibility of a witness giving evidence out of the defendant's sight. A judge may permit a witness to give evidence from behind a screen, but only if this will ensure that justice is, thereby, done. The judge must weigh up such factors as the importance of open justice, the possible risk of prejudice to the defendant and the needs of the witness. No adverse inference is to be drawn by the jury from the use of a screen (*R v Foster* (1995); see also *R v X,Y,Z* (1990). Further, a judge may, in a sexual offence case, allow a witness to be accompanied by a representative of a victim support group (*R v Lynch* (1993) and see Cross & Tapper (1995), p.249). Also, the anonymity of victim provisions which have applied to rape, now, by the Sexual Offences (Amendment) Act 1992, apply to many other sexual offences, including intercourse with a 'defective', procurement of a 'defective', as well as procurement of a woman by threats, by false pretences and by administering drugs and the under age sex offences.

Fourthly, there is no longer a requirement that a judge must give a warning of the danger of conviction in sexual cases where there is no supporting (or corroborative) evidence other than the evidence of the victim. However, where the witness is a mental patient detained through the criminal justice system, corroborative evidence is required and cannot come from another such witness (*R v Spencer* (1987)). This has little impact if any, upon evidence being given by people with learning difficulties. However, a warning can be given by a judge in a particular case, despite the abolition (by the Criminal Justice and Public Order Act 1994) of the requirement to give a warning. A warning is most likely to be given in a case involving sexual misconduct, especially where the only evidence is from a person with learning difficulties (see Blackstones' Criminal Practice 1996 (1996), para F5.4 and Cross & Tapper (1995), Chapter 5). A conviction is still possible without supporting evidence, but this issue is a factor which may have to be considered. A prosecution and conviction may be more likely where there is some supporting evidence such as the results of DNA profiling which can identify that a particular person had sexual intercourse with the victim.

Where the witness is a child, there are special rules assisting him/her to give evidence (see Cross & Tapper (1995), pp 229-233; and see Spencer & Flin (1993) and McEwan (1990)). In brief, they are:

i)   the evidence of a child is given unsworn and the only issue is the child's competence which is determined after the child begins to testify

ii)   the child's evidence may be presented through a videotaped interview (and the interview may itself enable an assessment of the child's competence)

iii)   if the child is to give evidence at the trial (and s/he must be available for cross examination even where her/his evidence-in-chief has been given via a videotaped interview), that evidence may be given through a live television link

iv)   in addition to common law powers to maintain the anonymity of a witness (see *R v Taylor & Crabb* (1995)), statute provides that children's identities must not be revealed where so ordered by the judge

v) a social worker may sit near to a child and speak to them without the jury being able to hear what is said, but the social worker should say as little as possible (*R v Smith* (1994)).

The recommendation of the Pigot Report (1989) that the use of videotaped interviews and live television links should be available to other vulnerable witnesses seems unlikely to be adopted in the near future.

4.8   Alternative methods of resolution

Since the law by its usual methods of response may not always be able adequately to deal with sexual abuse, other avenues have to be sought. In addition to pursuing any available complaint procedures and questioning the registration of private establishments, the only alternative available appears to be considering the reception of the abused person into guardianship under the Mental Health Act 1983. It is undoubtedly the case that this appears to be heavy handed and unreasonably to be acting against the abused rather than the abuser, but if the only way of stopping the abuse is to remove the person with learning difficulties from the situation where they are being abused and this cannot be done with that person's consent, this power, perhaps along with other Mental Health Act powers including admission to hospital, must be considered. A brief summary of reception into guardianship under the Mental Health Act 1983 follows. For further information and consideration of this power, see Fisher (1989); Gunn (1986) and the Mental Health Act Code of Practice, section 13. For consideration of the Mental Health Act generally, see Gostin (1983); Gostin (1986); Hoggett (1990) and Jones (1994).

4.9   Mental Health Act guardianship

A person may be received into guardianship if the conditions of s. 7 of the Mental Health Act 1983 are satisfied (and the relevant procedure is properly complied with). These are that they are at least 16 and suffers from one of the four specific forms of mental disorder, that is mental illness, severe mental impairment, mental impairment or psychopathic disorder, which must be of a nature of degree which warrants reception into guardianship; and that it must be necessary in the interests of the welfare of the 'patient' or for the protection of other persons that the 'patient' should be so received.

The guardian then has certain powers as listed in s.8 of the Mental Health Act 1983. These require the 'patient' to reside at a place specified by the authority or person named as guardian and to attend at places and times so specified for the purpose of medical treatment, occupation, education or training. They also require access to the 'patient' to be given, at any place where they are residing, to any doctor, approved social worker or other person so specified.

In fact, guardianship will not be available in any case for many people with learning difficulties since they will not suffer from either mental impairment or severe mental impairment (nor will many suffer additionally from mental illness or psychopathic disorder). This is primarily because the concepts require the person's conduct to be abnormally aggressive or seriously irresponsible, which will not often be the case. This can be seen from the definitions of the two concepts:

' "severe mental impairment" means a state of arrested or incomplete development of mind which includes severe impairment of intelligence and social functioning and is associated with abnormally aggressive or seriously irresponsible conduct on the part of the person concerned...'

' "mental impairment" means a state of arrested or incomplete development of mind (not amounting to severe mental impairment) which includes significant impairment of intelligence and social functioning and is associated with abnormally aggressive or seriously irresponsible conduct on the part of the person concerned ...'

4.10   The future: reform?

The Law Commission has made a number of proposals concerned with the public protection of vulnerable people at risk (Law Commission (1995)). Should these proposals be introduced a range of protective powers would be available to enable the investigation of allegations and short term protective action to be taken (see Gunn (1995), pp 220-222). The proposals do not address the concerns related to the criminal justice system identified at section 4.7.

References

Cases

B v Croydon Health Authority [1995] 1 All England Law Reports 683

Re B (a minor)(wardship: sterilization) [1987] 2 All England Law Reports 206

R v Bellamy (1985) 82 Criminal Appeal Reports 222

R v Blair (1995) unreported

R v Brown [1993] 2 All England Law Reports 75

Re C (1993) 149 New Law Journal Law Reports 1642

R v Chainey [1914] 1 Law Reports: King's Bench 137

Chatterton v Gerson [1981] 1 All England Law Reports 257

R v Court [1988] 2 All England Law Reports 221

Re D (a minor)(wardship: sterilisation) [1976] Law Reports: Family 185

R v Deakin [1994] 4 All England Law Reports 769

R v Donovan [1934] 2 Law Reports: King's Bench 498

R v Elbekkay [1995] Criminal Law Review 163

Re Eve (1986) 31 Dominion Law Reports (4th series) 1

Re F [1990] 1 Law Reports: Appeal Cases 1

R v Flattery (1877) 13 Cox's Criminal Cases 388

R v Foster [1995] Criminal Law Review 333

Gillick v Wisbech Area Health Authority [1985] 3 All England Law Reports 402

R v Hall (1987) 86 Criminal Appeal Reports 159

R v Hampshire [1995] 2 All England Law Reports 1019

R v Harling [1938] 1 All England Law Reports 307

R v Howard [1965] 3 All England Law Reports 684

R v Kowalski (1987) 86 Criminal Appeal Reports 339

R v Linekar [1995] 3 All England Law Reports 69

R v Lynch [1993] Criminal Law Review 868

R v Masih [1986] Criminal Law Review 395

Masterson v Holden [1986] 3 All England Law Reports 39

R v Newington [1990] Criminal Law Review 593

R v Olugboja (1981) 67 Criminal Appeal Reports 364

Re P (a minor) [1986] 1 Family Law Reports 272

Practice Note (Official Solicitor: Sterilisation) [1990] 2 Family Law Reports 530

Re R (a minor)(wardship: medical treatment) [1992] Law Reports: Family 11

R v R [1991] 2 All England Law Reports 257

R v Reakes [1974] Criminal Law Review 615

R v Robbins [1988] Criminal Law Review 744

R v Robinson [1994] 3 All England Law Reports 346

Re SG (a patient) (1990) Butterworths Medical Law Reports 95

R v Smith [1994] Criminal Law Review 458

R v Spencer [1987] Law Reports: Appeal Cases 128

Sidaway v Governors of Royal Bethlem and Maudsley Hospital [1985] 1 All England Law Reports 643

Re T (adult)(refusal of medical treatment) [1992] 4 All England Law Reports 649

R v Taylor & Crabb [1995] Criminal Law Review 253

Re W (a minor)(medical treatment) [1992] 4 All England Law Reports 627

R v X, Y, Z (1990) 91 Criminal Appeal Reports 36

Codes

'Code for Crown Prosecutors', see *Blackstone's Criminal Practice*, Appendix 5, 1996

Department of Health and Welsh Office, *Mental Health Act 1983: code of practice*, 1993

Reports

Home Office, *Report of the advisory group on video evidence*, Chair: His Honour Judge Thomas Pigot, 1989

Law Commission (1990b), *Rape within marriage*, Working paper no. 11

Law Commission (1995), *Mental incapacity*, Report no. 231

Books

Bailey S H and Gunn M J, *Smith and Bailey on the Modern English legal system*, Sweet and Maxwell, 3rd ed, 1996

Murphy P (ed), *Blackstone's Criminal Practice 1996*, Blackstone's Press 1996

Card R, *Card, Cross and Jones on Criminal Law*, Butterworths, 13th ed, 1995

Cretney S M and Masson J M, *Principles of Family Law*, Sweet and Maxwell, 5th ed, 1990

Cross R and Tapper C, *The law of evidence*, Butterworths, 7th ed, 1995

DHSS, *Memorandum on the Mental Health Act 1983*, HMSO, 1987

Encyclopedia of social services law and practice, Butterworths (looseleaf)

Fortson R, *The law on the misuse of drugs*, Sweet and Maxwell, 1988

Gostin L O, *A practical guide to mental health law*, MIND, 1983

Gostin L O, *Mental health services – law and practice*, Shaw & Sons, 1986 (looseleaf)

Hoggett B M, *Mental health law.* Sweet and Maxwell, 3rd ed, 1990

Honore T, *Sex law*, Duckworth, 1978

Jones R M, *Mental Health Act manual*, Sweet and Maxwell, 4th ed, 1994

Kennedy I & Grubb A, *Medical law: text and materials*, Butterworths, 2nd ed, 1994

Lyon C M, *The law relating to children*, Butterworths,1993

Smith J C & Hogan B, *Criminal Law*, Butterworths, 7th ed, 1992

Spencer J R & Flin R, *The evidence of children*, Blackstone Press, 2nd ed 1993

Temkin J, *Rape and the legal process*, Sweet and Maxwell, 1987

Articles

Carson D, 'Legal issues' in Carson, D. (ed), *The law and the sexuality of people with mental handicap,* University of Southampton, 1987

Fisher M, 'Guardianship under the Mental Health Act', *The Journal of Social Welfare Law,* 1988, pp316-327

Gunn M J, 'Mental Health Act guardianship: where now?', *The Journal of Social Welfare Law,* 1986, pp155-152

Gunn M J, 'Treatment and mental handicap', *The Anglo-American Law Review,* 16, 1987 pp242-267

Gunn M J, 'Sex and the law for people with mental handicap and for staff' in Wynn-Jones, A (ed), *Mentally handicapped people coping with relationships,* Blackstone Press, 1988

Gunn M J, 'Sexual abuse and adults with mental handicap: can the law help?' in Brown H and Craft A (eds), *Thinking the unthinkable,* Family Planning Association, 1989

Gunn M J, 'Consent to treatment', *The Journal of Forensic Psychiatry,* 1, 1990, pp81-87

Gunn M J, 'The meaning of incapacity', *Medical Law Review,* 2, 1994, pp8-29

Gunn M J , 'Mental incapacity – the Law Commission's report', *Child and Family Law Quarterly,* 7, pp209-222

McEwan J, 'In the box or on the box? The Pigot Report and child witnesses', *The Criminal Law Review,* 1990, pp363-370

Morgan D, 'F v West Berkshire Health Authority', *The Journal of Social Welfare Law,* 1990, pp204-211

Shaw J, 'Sterilisation of mentally handicapped people: judges riles OK?', *The Modern Law Review,* 53, 1990, pp91-106

Smith J C, 'Commentary to R v C', *The Criminal Law Review,* 1991.

Useful addresses

FPA (national office)
2-12 Pentonville Road
London N1 9FP.
Tel 0171 837 5432

FPA Cymru
4 Museum Place
Cardiff CF1 3BG.
Tel 01222 342766

Provides information and
resources on contraception, sex
education and sexual health
issues. Offers training and
consultancy for professionals in a
range of settings including those
working with people with
learning difficulties. Runs a
helpline on contraception and
sexual health matters.

**British Institute of Learning
Disabilities (BILD)**
Information and Resource Centre
Wolverhampton Rd
Worcestershire DY10 3PP.
Tel 01562 850251

Provides information on new
developments in the learning
difficulties field, plus resources
and reading lists.

Children's Legal Centre,
University of Essex, Wivenhoe Park,
Colchester, Essex CO4 3SQ.
Tel 01206 873820

Lobbies on law and policy issues
concerning children and young
people. Offers free advice and
information by letter and
telephone and produces
publications.

Health Education Authority
Hamilton House
Mabledon Place
London WC1H 9TX.
Tel 0171 383 3833

Runs research work and pilot
projects, offers training advice,
leaflets and posters, free
resources list.

Health Promotion Wales
Ffynnon las, Ty-Glas Avenue,
Cardiff CF5 5DZ.
Tel 01222 752222

Runs research work and pilot
projects, is a central contact for
district health promotion
departments.

**MENCAP (Royal Society for
Mentally Handicapped
Children and Adults)**
National Centre
123 Golden Lane
London EC1 3PP.
Tel 0171 454 0454

Offers campaigning advice,
holiday service, employment
opportunities and residential
homes for those with learning
difficulties.

**MIND (National Association fo
Mental Health)**
Granta House, Broadway,
London E15 4BQ.
Tel 0181 519 2122

Offers training, information and
advocacy services on mental
health issues.

NAPSAC (National Association for the Protection from Sexual Abuse of Adults and Children with learning disabilities)
Department of Learning Disabilities,
Floor E, South Block
University of Nottingham Medical School
Queen's Medical Centre
Nottingham NG7 2UH.
Tel 01602 709987

Offers information and training and produces a quarterly bulletin. Has a membership network.

People First
Instrument House
207-215 King's Cross Road
London WC1X 9DB.
Tel 0171 713 6400

A self-advocacy group. Offers training and resources.

SENJIT (Special Education Needs Joint Initiative for Training)
University of London
Institute of Education
20 Bedford Way
London WC1H 0AL.
Tel 0171 612 6273

Provides guidelines for sex education and publications for INSET and special educational needs.

Special Needs Sexuality Project
Ladywell Leisure Centre
261 Lewisham High Street
London SE13 6NS.
Tel 0181 690 7438

Offers advice, information and booklets on sex education issues for those with learning difficulties, their parents and carers.

SPOD (The Association to Aid the Sexual and Personal Relationships of People with a Disability)
286 Camden Road
London N7 0BJ.
Tel 0171 607 8851/2

Offers information and advice for people and their carers. Provides books and leaflets.